Pasta

Pappardelle caprese, p. 28

Fresh pasta with beans, p. 50

Ravioli with olive pesto, p. 90

Penne with gorgonzola, p. 166

Farfalle with peas & ham, p. 198

Spaghetti with meatballs, p. 306

Spaghetti with tuna & capers, p. 286

Spicy spaghetti with pancetta & onion, p. 278

Spaghetti with zucchini & peppers, p. 258

CARLA BARDI

Pasta

Delicious Recipes for a Healthy Life

Reader's Digest

THE READER'S DIGEST ASSOCIATION, INC.
New York, New York / Montreal / Singapore

A READER'S DIGEST BOOK
This edition published by
The Reader's Digest Association, Inc.
by arrangement with McRae Books Srl

This book was created and produced by
McRae Books Srl
via Umbria, 36 - 50145 Florence, Italy
info@mcraebooks.com

FOR MCRAE BOOKS
Project Director Anne McRae
Art Director Marco Nardi
Photography Brent Parker Jones (R&R
PhotoStudio)
Text Carla Bardi
Dietitian Penny Doyle
Editing Lesley Robb
Food Styling Lee Blaylock
Layouts Aurora Granata
Prepress Filippo Delle Monache, Davide
Gasparri

FOR READER'S DIGEST
U.S. Project Editor: Andrea Chesman
Canadian Project Manager:
Pamela Johnson
Senior Art Director: George McKeon
Executive Editor, Trade Publishing:
Dolores York
Associate Publisher, Trade Publishing:
Rosanne McManus
President and Publisher, Trade Publishing:
Harold Clarke

LIBRARY OF CONGRESS
CATALOGING-IN-PUBLICATION DATA

Bardi, Carla.
  Pasta / Carla Bardi.
      p. cm.
    ISBN 978-1-60652-195-3 (U.S. edition)
    ISBN 978-1-60652-196-0 (international
  edition)
1. International cookery. I. Bardi, Carla. II, III.
  Title.
  TX837.M677 2010
  641.5'636–dc22

                                          2010004578

We are committed to both the quality of
our products and the service we provide to
our customers. We value your comments,
so please feel free to contact us.

    The Reader's Digest Association, Inc.
    Adult Trade Publishing
    Reader's Digest Road
    Pleasantville, NY 10570-7000

For more Reader's Digest products and
information, visit our websites:

    www.rd.com (in the United States)
    www.readersdigest.ca (in Canada)
    www.rdasia.com (in Asia)

Printed in China

1 3 5 7 9 10 8 6 4 2

NOTE TO OUR READERS
Eating eggs or egg whites that are not
completely cooked poses the possibility of
salmonella food poisoning. The risk is
greater for pregnant women, the elderly, the
very young, and persons with impaired
immune systems. If you are concerned
about salmonella, you can use reconstituted
powdered egg whites or pasteurized eggs.

The level of difficulty for each recipe is given on a scale from
1 (easy) to 3 (complicated).

Contents

Introduction

Pasta is a key dish in the super-healthy Mediterranean diet. Served with fresh or sautéed vegetables, seafood, extra-virgin olive oil, and a grating of Parmesan cheese, it packs as much goodness as it does flavor and energy.

Almost everyone loves pasta, making it the perfect food both for family meals and entertaining. It can be adapted to the season, with cool pasta salads ideal for summer and hearty lasagne and baked pasta great in the winter months. It is versatile, with lots of dishes that can be prepared ahead of time and either served chilled or quickly cooked as required. And for those who are watching their budget, remember that even the best imported brands are well within the average family's purse strings.

In this book we have chosen more than 140 classic and modern recipes from the Italian repertoire. In the first chapter we have included instructions for making fresh pasta at home. But we have also edited the recipes so that you can buy fresh tagliatelle and serve them with the sauces we suggest. Here you will find a host of exquisite pasta dishes, with something for every occasion. Buon appetito!

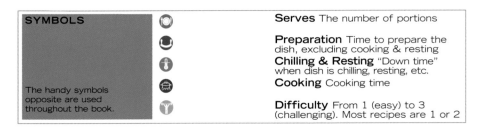

SYMBOLS

The handy symbols opposite are used throughout the book.

Serves The number of portions

Preparation Time to prepare the dish, excluding cooking & resting

Chilling & Resting "Down time" when dish is chilling, resting, etc.

Cooking Cooking time

Difficulty From 1 (easy) to 3 (challenging). Most recipes are 1 or 2

opposite: farfalle with peas & ham, p. 198

choosing a pasta dish

This book has more than 140 recipes for delicious pasta dishes—something for everyone, and every occasion. But, what if you only have a few minutes or just a handful of ingredients in the refrigerator? The QUICK & EASY section below will solve the first problem and the JUST A FEW INGREDIENTS on page 14 will solve the second. Looking for an old favorite? See our CLASSICS suggestions. See also the LOW COST, CHALLENGING, HEALTHY CHOICE, and EDITOR'S CHOICE recommendations.

QUICK & EASY

spaghetti with tomato & lemon, p. 254

pasta with tomatoes, ricotta & pesto, p. 144

penne with ricotta, zucchini & orange, p. 154

ruote with pesto & cherry tomatoes, p. 152

tagliolini with almond & basil pesto, p. 32

ravioli with olive pesto, p. 90

spirals with beans & pesto, p. 150

maccheroni with onion
sauce, p. 138

cool fusilli with tomatoes
& onion, p. 120

spaghetti with lemon
& olives, p. 232

bucatini with tomatoes,
almonds & fried bread,
p. 274

homemade spaghetti with tomato & garlic sauce, p. 56

CHALLENGING

pappardelle with duck
ragù, p. 72

whole-wheat spaghetti with
spicy tomato ragù, p. 52

fried spaghetti parcels, p. 312

lasagne with meatballs,
p. 108

lasagne with pumpkin,
p. 110

pappardelle with rosemary,
p. 30

homemade spaghetti
with garlic & oil, p. 54

spaghetti with ricotta
& pecorino, p. 226

spaghetti with zucchini,
p. 246

tagliatelle with roasted tomato sauce, p. 40

HEALTHY CHOICE

pizzocheri with cabbage,
p. 104

penne with cherry
tomatoes, p. 140

whole-wheat spaghetti with summer vegetables, p. 256

farfalle with shrimp
& pesto, p. 178

pasta salad with tuna
& olives, p. 128

spinach & ricotta cannelloni with tomato sauce, p. 214

linguine with pesto, potatoes & beans, p. 240

spaghetti with clams, p. 288

bucatini with amatriciana sauce, p. 272

spaghetti with squid's ink, p. 284

EDITOR'S CHOICE

pasta squares with tomatoes & pancetta, p. 34

pasta salad with baby mozzarella & tomatoes, p. 124

lasagne stacks with pesto, p. 106

penne with swordfish & salmon, p. 188

fusilli with fish cakes, p. 184

penne with tomatoes & goat cheese, p. 156

spaghetti with bell peppers & pancetta, p. 260

Homemade
Fresh Pasta

fresh pasta:
just eggs & flour

Preparing pasta at home is a lot simpler than you may think. In this chapter we explain how to make pasta dough and how to roll it through a machine to achieve the desired thickness. For those without a pasta machine, or with a hankering for perfection, we have also explained how to roll pasta by hand. Cutting pasta is simple and we have explained how to do it both by hand and using a machine.

With its delicate texture and flavor, homemade pasta is a unique product that requires special care and attention. The first thing you will notice is that even if you make pasta often, some days the dough will require less flour or more kneading, or other small changes to the basic method. Even slight variations in temperature and humidity, or in your own mood, can affect the outcome. For this reason we strongly suggest that you always mix and knead the dough by hand even if you use a pasta machine to roll and cut. This will allow you to modify the dough each time, correcting the amount of flour or egg and judging the time required for kneading.

Plain pasta is made with unbleached or all-purpose (plain) flour, but many other types of flour can be used. Each one will require more or less liquid; refer to the chart on the next page for quantities and then adjust them as you work. Kneading time will also vary depending on the flour you use. Soft-wheat flour has less gluten and takes the longest time to knead, generally about 20 minutes. Hard-wheat flour will take about half that time.

With regard to quantity, you should normally allow about $3\frac{1}{2}$ ounces (100 g) of fresh pasta per person. Each portion has $3\frac{1}{2}$ ounces (100 g) of flour and one large egg (as the pasta dries it will lose a little weight). In Italy, where pasta is eaten every day, it is served as a first course and followed by an often substantial second course. If you are serving pasta as the main part of the meal, you can increase the quantities.

Always cook fresh pasta in a large saucepan of already salted, boiling water. For every $3\frac{1}{2}$ ounces (100 g) of pasta, you should allow 4 cups (1 liter) of water and $1\frac{1}{2}$ teaspoons of coarse sea salt. If the fresh pasta has become very dry, it is better to add the salt after the pasta, when the water returns to a boil. Cooking times depend on the shape and thickness of the pasta. Simple ribbon pasta rolled through the machine to the thinnest setting will require only 2 minutes to cook. Thicker or filled pasta such as tortellini will require a few minutes more.

Many types of pasta can be frozen. Lay nests of ribbon pasta or pieces of filled pasta well spaced on a large tray and place in the freezer. Transfer to bags as soon as they are frozen and seal. Filled pasta with potato filling is not suited to freezing. Baked pasta can be prepared up to just before baking. To thaw, remove from the freezer and bake in a warm oven for 30 minutes.

DOUGH	ALL-PURPOSE FLOUR	OTHER FLOUR	EGGS	WATER	OTHER INGREDIENTS	SALT
Plain fresh pasta	2⅔ cups (400 g)		4			
Durum or hard wheat pasta		2⅔ cups (400 g) durum or hard wheat		1¼ cups/ 300 ml		
Durum or hard wheat and egg pasta	1⅓ cups (200 g)	1⅓ cups (200 g) durum or hard wheat	4			
Ravioli pasta	2⅓ cups (350 g)		3	2 tbsp		
Whole-wheat / wholemeal pasta	1⅓ cups (200 g)	1⅓ cups (200 g) whole-wheat	4			
Chestnut pasta	2 cups (300 g)	⅔ cup (100 g) chestnut	2	4 tbsp		1 pinch
Buckwheat pasta		2 cups (300 g) buck-wheat & ⅔ cup (100 g) durum or hard wheat		scant cup / 200 ml		
Colored pasta (tomato, spinach, Swiss chard, etc.)	2⅓ cups (350 g)		3		⅓ cup (50 g) purée	1 pinch
Aromatic (coffee, herb, chocolate, etc.)	2⅓ cups (350 g)		4		⅓ cup (50 g) powder or minced herbs	
Black	2⅔ cups (400 g)		3		1 tbsp squid's ink (about 3 sacs)	

Note: If you prefer to make whole-wheat (wholemeal), colored, aromatic, or other kinds of pasta, use the ingredients in the quantities given and follow the instructions in the following pages. You will get about 14 ounces (400 g) of pasta, enough for 4 servings.

preparing the dough

Plain fresh pasta is made of a simple mixture of artfully kneaded flour and eggs. In Italy, soft wheat "0" flour is used. All-purpose (plain) white flour can be used in other parts of the world. Fresh pasta can also be made with hard wheat, buckwheat, chestnut, or other types of flour, and the eggs can be replaced with water, oil, or milk. Whatever the ingredients, the basic method is always the same.

INGREDIENTS

2⅔ cups (400 g) all-purpose (plain) flour
4   very fresh large eggs

EGGS
Always use very fresh eggs. They should be at room temperature. The recipes in this book are all based on large (2-ounce/60-g) eggs.

1. **Sift the flour** onto a clean work surface (preferably made of wood) and shape into a mound. Make a hollow in the center.

2. **Use a fork** to beat the eggs lightly in a small bowl. Pour the beaten eggs into the hollow center of the mound of flour.

3. **Use the fork** to gradually incorporate the eggs into the flour. Take care not to break the wall of flour or the eggs will run.

4. When almost all the flour has been absorbed use your hands and, if you have one, a pasta scraper to gather the dough up into a ball.

5. Wash and dry your hands and begin the kneading process. Place the dough on a clean work surface. At first it will be rough and grainy.

6. Knead by pushing down and forward on the ball of pasta with the heel of your palm. Fold the dough in half, give it a quarter-turn, and repeat.

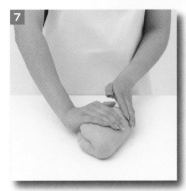

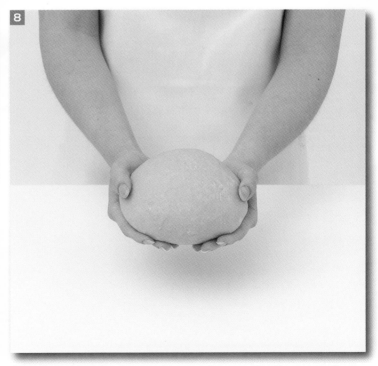

7. As you work the dough will become smoother. The warmth of your hands and the rhythmic kneading creates a gluten-forming protein, which gives pasta its special texture.

KNEADING TIME
This depends on: 1) type of flour; 2) kneading skill; 3) temperature and humidity. Soft wheat dough usually takes 20 minutes, a mixed soft and hard wheat dough 15 minutes, and hard wheat dough 10 minutes.

8. After 10–20 minutes (depending on the flour used), the dough should be smooth and silky, with tiny air bubbles visible on the surface. Wrap the dough in plastic wrap (cling film) and let rest for 30 minutes.

rolling and cutting the dough by machine

If making simple ribbon pasta, such as fettuccine or lasagna, run all the sheets through the machine one notch at a time. This will give them time to dry a little before being rolled to the next thickness. If making stuffed pasta, such as ravioli, roll the pasta one sheet at a time to the thinnest setting and make the ravioli before rolling the next sheet. This will prevent the pasta from drying out too much.

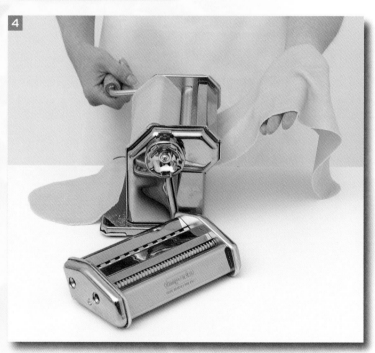

2. Roll a piece of dough through the machine at the thickest setting.

1. Divide the dough into 5–6 pieces (for 14 ounces/400 g of pasta, enough for 4 people).

3. Continue rolling the dough through the machine, reducing the thickness setting one notch at a time down to the required thickness. You may need to fold the pasta as you work to obtain an evenly shaped sheet.

4. The finished pasta sheets should be smooth and evenly shaped, without any folds. Extremely long sheets are difficult to manage; don't make them any longer than about 12–14 inches (30–35 cm).

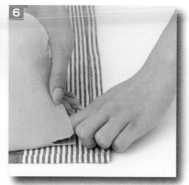

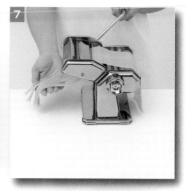

5. Sprinkle the finished sheets with semolina and cover with a clean dry cloth. This will allow them to dry a little before you begin to cut them.

6. To test the pasta to see if it is ready to cut, insert your index finger into a fold of pasta and pull slightly. If the pasta stretches it is not ready; if it tears, it is ready to cut.

7. Set the machine to the width required (for tagliolini, tagliatelle, pappardelle, etc.) and run each sheet through. If making ribbon pasta, gather the pasta up in your hand as it comes out of the machine and shape into little "nests."

RIBBON PASTA
Classic Italian fresh ribbon pasta types are named according to their approximate width. The narrowest ribbons, taglierini or tagliolini, are about ¼ inch (5–6 mm) wide. Tagliatelle (also known as fettuccine) are normally about ½ inch (1 cm) wide, while pappardelle measure about 1 inch (2.5 cm) in width.

TAGLIATELLE

PAPPARDELLE

TAGLIOLINI

CHOCOLATE
TAGLIATELLE

TOMATO
TAGLIATELLE

TOMATO
TAGLIOLINI

rolling the dough by hand

Pasta machines are ideal for new pasta makers, but as you gain in experience you may also wish to try rolling the pasta by hand. When properly done, hand-rolled pasta is better than the machine-rolled variety. Rolling by hand requires lots of energy and a large, flat work surface, preferably made of wood. You will also need a very long, rather thin rolling pin made especially for pasta.

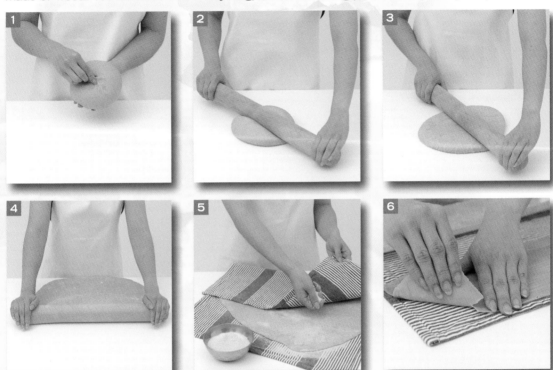

1. Unwrap the ball of pasta and use your fingertips to pull up a "button" or smaller ball of pasta on the top. This will keep the center piece of the pasta as thick as the edges when you roll.

2. Put the ball of pasta on a large clean work surface. Place the rolling pin on top and begin rolling from the center.

3. Keep rolling the pasta by exerting an even pressure all along the length of the pin. Give the pasta a quarter-turn from time to time and keep working.

4. Wrap the pasta around the rolling pin and continue rolling backward and forward, running your hands along the pin. When the sheet of pasta is as large as the work surface, let half of it drape over the edge of the table or board and keep rolling.

5. Dust the finished sheets with semolina or coarsely ground cornmeal and cover with a clean dry cloth. This will allow the pasta to dry a little before you begin to cut it.

6. To test the pasta to see if it is ready to cut, try to tear it gently. If the pasta stretches, it is not ready; if it tears, it is ready to cut.

cutting pasta by hand

Pasta machines can cut lasagna and all the simple ribbon pasta types, such as tagliatelle and pappardelle, but even if you do own a machine, you may want to cut some ribbon pasta shapes by hand to give them that special "homemade look." Always remember to let the pasta dry a little in a floured cloth before cutting.

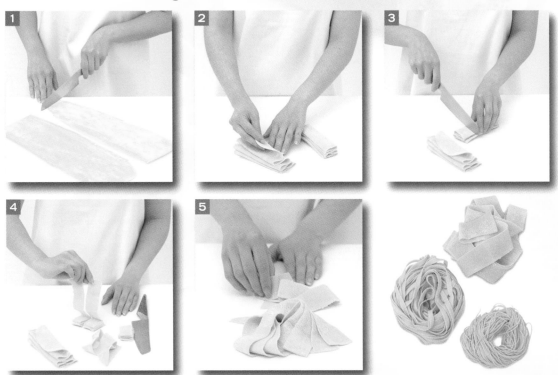

1. Lasagna: The pasta will come out of the machine in sheets measuring about 6 x 12 inches (14 x 30 cm). Cut into 5 x 6-inch (13 x 15-cm) rectangles.

2. Ribbon pasta (pappardelle, fettuccine, taglierini, tagliolini, etc): Place the pasta sheets on a clean work surface sprinkled with semolina or coarsely ground cornmeal and fold them into flat rolls. Leave a border of about 1 inch (2.5 cm) sticking out from the roll.

3. Use a sharp knife to cut the ribbon pasta to the desired width. The narrowest ribbons, taglierini or tagliolini, are about $1/4$ inch (5 mm) wide. Fettuccine (also known as tagliatelle) are normally about $1/2$ inch (1 cm) wide, while pappardelle can be up to 1 inch (2.5 cm) in width.

4. To unfold the ribbon pasta, grasp 2–3 pieces of the pasta sticking out from the roll and lift them up. Shape into "nests" or lie in flat strips on a floured cloth.

5. Finished pappardelle can be quite wide.

Fresh Pasta

pappardelle caprese

With fresh tomatoes, mozzarella, and basil, this "caprese" condiment is inspired by the salad of the same name from the Italian island of Capri. It is perfect for a quick and nutritious weekday dinner.

Serves 4

10 minutes

Time for pasta

3–4 minutes

1

14 ounces (400 g) fresh pappardelle, homemade (see pages 16–25), or store-bought

4 plum or vine-ripened tomatoes, diced

½ cup (50 g) coarsely chopped fresh basil leaves

5 ounces (150 g) mozzarella cheese, diced

1 tablespoon capers, rinsed and drained

3 tablespoons extra-virgin olive oil

1 tablespoon balsamic or red wine vinegar

Shaved fresh Parmesan cheese (optional)

Freshly ground black pepper

1. **If using homemade pasta,** prepare the pappardelle following the instructions on pages 16–25.

2. **Cook** the pappardelle in a large pot of salted boiling water until al dente, 3–4 minutes. Drain and place in a large bowl.

3. **While the pasta is cooking,** combine the tomatoes, basil, mozzarella, capers, oil, and vinegar in a medium bowl.

4. **Add** the tomato mixture to the hot pasta and toss gently.

5. **Divide** the pasta evenly among four heated serving bowls. If using, sprinkle with a few Parmesan cheese shavings and season with pepper.

AMOUNT PER SERVING NUTRITION FACTS PERCENT DAILY VALUES (based on 2000 calories)	593 CALORIES 28%	23g PROTEIN 50%	23g FAT 28%	4g FIBER 16%	79g CARBS 61%	0.5g SALT 10%

If you liked this recipe, you will love these as well.

lasagna stacks with pesto

106

farfalle salad with cherry tomatoes & olives

114

pappardelle with rosemary

Rosemary's intense aromatic flavor works deliciously well with the garlic in this dish. To prepare the rosemary, strip the leaves from the woody stems and chop finely.

- Serves 4
- 10 minutes
- Time for pasta
- 25 minutes

2

14 ounces (400 g) fresh pappardelle, homemade (see pages 16–25), or store-bought
4 cloves garlic, finely chopped
1 tablespoon finely chopped fresh rosemary

$\frac{1}{4}$ cup (60 g) butter, cubed
1 beef bouillon (stock) cube
Freshly grated Parmesan cheese, to serve

1. **If using homemade pasta,** prepare the pappardelle following the instructions on pages 16–25.

2. **Put** the garlic and rosemary in a small saucepan with the butter. Simmer over low heat, stirring often, until the butter is golden brown and the garlic has softened, about 4 minutes.

3. **Crumble** the bouillon cube into the mixture and stir until it is completely dissolved.

4. **Cook** the pappardelle in a large pot of salted boiling water until al dente, 3–4 minutes. Add 3 tablespoons of the cooking water to the butter sauce.

5. **Drain** the pasta and put in a heated serving bowl. Pour the sauce over the top and toss gently. Serve hot with Parmesan cheese.

AMOUNT PER SERVING	558	18g	22g	3g	77g	0.5g
NUTRITION FACTS	CALORIES	PROTEIN	FAT	FIBER	CARBS	SALT
PERCENT DAILY VALUES (based on 2000 calories)	27%	39%	27%	12%	59%	10%

If you liked this recipe, you will love these as well.

lasagna with pumpkin

110

spaghetti with zucchini

246

spaghettini with fresh herbs

248

tagliolini with almond & basil pesto

Pine nuts are the traditional nutty ingredient in pesto, but almonds add an extra creaminess. Almonds are a good source of protein, fiber, and vitamin E. They also contain antioxidants that may help prevent cancer, heart disease, and Alzheimer's.

Serves 4

15 minutes

Time for pasta

2–3 minutes

1

14 ounces (400 g) fresh tagliolini or angel hair pasta, homemade (see pages 16–25), or store-bought

¾ cup (120 g) blanched almonds, finely chopped

1 clove garlic, finely chopped
Salt

1 large bunch fresh basil

1 large ripe tomato, peeled, seeds removed, and chopped

1 dried chile, crumbled, or ½ teaspoon dried red pepper flakes

3 tablespoons extra-virgin olive oil

1. **If using homemade pasta,** prepare the tagliolini following the instructions on pages 16–25.

2. **Chop** the almonds, garlic, and a pinch of salt in a food processor until almost smooth.

3. **Add** the basil and tomato and chop until smooth. Season with salt, chile, and oil. Put in a large serving dish.

4. **Cook** the pasta in a large pot of salted boiling water until al dente, 2–3 minutes.

5. **Drain well,** reserving 2–3 tablespoons of the cooking water. Add the pasta to the serving dish with the sauce, adding the reserved cooking water if the sauce is too dry. Toss gently and serve hot.

AMOUNT PER SERVING	596	20g	28g	5g	70	1.8g
NUTRITION FACTS	**CALORIES**	**PROTEIN**	**FAT**	**FIBER**	**CARBS**	**SALT**
PERCENT DAILY VALUES (based on 2 000 calories)	29%	43%	35%	20%	54%	33%

If you liked this recipe, you will love these as well.

fettuccine with pine nut & walnut pesto

38

ruote with pesto and cherry tomatoes

152

spaghetti with walnut pesto

228

pasta squares with tomatoes & pancetta

Pancetta is an Italian deli meat that is cured with salt, pepper, and other spices, but is not smoked. It is generally sold rolled up into sausage shapes.

Serves 4

40 minutes

90 minutes

40 minutes

2

PASTA DOUGH

2 cups (300 g) all-purpose (plain) flour

²/₃ cup (100 g) stone-ground cornmeal (fine polenta)

¼ teaspoon salt

²/₃ cup (150 ml) lukewarm water + more as needed

SAUCE

2 tablespoons extra-virgin olive oil

1 red onion, finely chopped

5 ounces (150 g) pancetta

1½ pounds (750 g) tomatoes, peeled and chopped and pressed through a fine-mesh strainer (passata)

Salt and freshly ground black pepper

4 tablespoons freshly grated aged pecorino cheese

1. **To prepare the pasta dough,** mound the flour, cornmeal, and salt up on a clean work surface and make a well in the center. Mix in enough water to make a smooth dough. Knead until smooth and elastic, 15–20 minutes, Shape the dough into a ball, wrap in plastic wrap (cling film), and let rest for 30 minutes.

2. **Roll out** the dough to ⅛ inch (3 mm) thick. Cut into 1-inch (2.5-cm) squares.

3. **To prepare the sauce,** heat the oil in a medium frying pan over low heat.

Add the onion and pancetta and sweat until the onion has softened, about 10 minutes.

4. **Stir in** the tomatoes, season with salt and pepper, and simmer over medium heat for 25 minutes.

5. **Meanwhile,** cook the pasta in a large pot of salted boiling water until al dente, 3–4 minutes.

6. **Drain well** and add to the sauce, tossing gently. Sprinkle with the pecorino and serve hot.

AMOUNT PER SERVING	540 CALORIES	22g PROTEIN	12g FAT	3g FIBER	91g CARBS	1.7g SALT
NUTRITION FACTS						
PERCENT DAILY VALUES (based on 2000 calories)	26%	48%	15%	12%	70%	31%

If you liked this recipe, you will love these as well.

penne with spicy tomato sauce

160

spaghetti with bell peppers & pancetta

260

bucatini with amatriciana sauce

272

fettuccine with cream & ham

If desired, try this dish with pretty green spinach fettuccine. To make spinach fettuccine, see the chart on page 19; it is made by adding about 2 ounces (50 g) of cooked, finely chopped spinach purée to the pasta dough.

 Serves 4

 15 minutes

 Time for pasta

 10 minutes

 1

14 ounces (400 g) fresh fettuccine, homemade (see pages 16–25), or store-bought

¼ cup (60 g) butter

4 ounces (125 g) ham, cut into thin strips

¾ cup (200 ml) light (single) cream

Salt and freshly ground white pepper

⅛ teaspoon freshly grated nutmeg

½ cup (60 g) freshly grated Parmesan cheese

1. **If using homemade pasta,** prepare the fettuccine following the instructions on pages 16–25.

2. **Melt** the butter in a large frying pan over medium heat. Add the ham and sauté until crisp, about 5 minutes.

3. **Pour in** the cream and simmer until thickened, 2–3 minutes. Season with salt, white pepper, and nutmeg.

4. **Cook** the pasta in a large pot of salted boiling water until al dente, 3–4 minutes.

5. **Drain well** and add to the pan with the sauce. Toss gently. Sprinkle with the Parmesan and serve hot.

AMOUNT PER SERVING	729	29g	35g	3g	80g	1.6g
NUTRITION FACTS	**CALORIES**	**PROTEIN**	**FAT**	**FIBER**	**CARBS**	**SALT**
PERCENT DAILY VALUES (based on 2000 calories)	35%	63%	43%	12%	62%	30%

If you liked this recipe, you will love these as well.

tortellini with woodcutter's sauce

98

farfalle with peas & ham

198

baked rigatoni with ham & mushrooms

218

fettuccine with pine nut & walnut pesto

Walnuts are rich in omega-3 fatty acids, vitamins B and E, and many minerals. They also contain melatonin, an antioxidant that promotes restful sleep.

 Serves 4

30 minutes

Time for pasta

10–15 minutes

1

14	ounces (400 g) fresh fettuccine, homemade (see pages 16–25), or store-bought
3	cups (400 g) walnuts, in shells
¼	cup (45 g) pine nuts

2	cloves garlic
1	cup (100 g) fresh parsley
⅓	cup (90 ml) extra-virgin olive oil
	Salt

1. **If using homemade pasta,** prepare the fettuccine following the instructions on pages 16–25.

2. **Preheat** the oven to 350°F (180°C/gas 4). Put the pine nuts on a baking sheet and roast until pale gold, 5–10 minutes.

3. **Shell** the walnuts and chop finely in a food processor with the pine nuts, garlic, parsley, and oil. Season with salt.

4. **Cook** the pasta in a large pot of salted boiling water until al dente, 3–4 minutes.

5. **Drain well** and put in a large heated serving dish. Cover with the sauce, toss carefully, and serve hot.

AMOUNT PER SERVING	980	24g	65g	5g	80g	2.1g
NUTRITION FACTS	CALORIES	PROTEIN	FAT	FIBER	CARBS	SALT
PERCENT DAILY VALUES (based on 2000 calories)	47%	52%	80%	20%	62%	38%

If you liked this recipe, you will love these as well.

tagliolini with almond & basil pesto

32

ruote with pesto & cherry tomatoes

152

spaghetti with walnut pesto

228

fettuccine with roasted tomato sauce

Oven-roasted tomatoes have a deliciously concentrated flavor and a wonderful texture. Rich in vitamin C and potassium, tomatoes also contain lycopene, a potent antioxidant that becomes stronger when cooked. It protects against cancer, heart disease, and many other illnesses.

 Serves 4

 15 minutes

 Time for pasta

 25–30 minutes

 2

14	ounces (400 g) fresh fettuccine, homemade (see pages 16–25), or store-bought
2	pounds (1 kg) firm, ripe tomatoes
2	cloves garlic, finely chopped
1/3	cup (90 ml) extra-virgin olive oil

1	tablespoon finely chopped fresh parsley
	Salt
	Fresh basil leaves, to serve

1. **If using homemade pasta,** prepare the fettuccine following the instructions on pages 16–25.

2. **Preheat** the oven to 400°F (200°C/gas 6). Cut the tomatoes in half and remove the seeds. Place the tomato shells upside-down on a baking sheet and bake until they have lost their excess water and the skins are burnt, 20–25 minutes.

3. **Let cool** a little, then slip off the skins and mash the flesh in a large bowl. Stir in the garlic, oil, parsley, and salt.

4. **Cook** the pasta in a large pot of salted boiling water until al dente, 3–4 minutes.

5. **Drain well** and put in a large heated serving dish. Add the sauce and basil and toss gently. Serve hot.

AMOUNT PER SERVING	650	18g	28g	6g	86g	0.2g
NUTRITION FACTS	CALORIES	PROTEIN	FAT	FIBER	CARBS	SALT
PERCENT DAILY VALUES (based on 2000 calories)	31%	39%	35%	24%	66%	4%

If you liked this recipe, you will love these as well.

whole-wheat spaghetti with spicy tomato sauce
52

maccheroni with tomatoes & speck
200

spaghetti with sun-dried tomatoes
262

fettuccine with artichokes

When buying artichokes, pick those with well-colored, undamaged, tightly closed leaves. If fresh, the artichoke should "squeak" when compressed.

Serves 6

30 minutes

Time for pasta

30 minutes

2

14	ounces (400 g) fresh whole-wheat (wholemeal) fettuccine, homemade (see pages 16–25), or store-bought
6	fresh artichokes
1	lemon
¼	cup (60 ml) extra-virgin olive oil
¼	cup (60 g) butter
2	cloves garlic, finely chopped
1	cup (250 ml) water, + extra, as required
	Salt and freshly ground black pepper
2	tablespoons finely chopped fresh parsley
1	cup (125 g) freshly grated pecorino cheese

1. If using homemade pasta, prepare the fettuccine following the instructions on pages 16–25.

2. Trim the stalks and cut the top third off the tops of the artichokes. Remove the tough outer leaves by bending them down and snapping them off. Cut in half and use a sharp knife to remove any fuzzy choke. Slice into thin wedges. Place in a medium bowl of cold water with the lemon juice.

3. Heat the oil and butter in a large frying pan over medium heat. Add the garlic and sauté until golden, 3–4 minutes.

4. Drain the artichokes and add to the pan. Sauté for 2–3 minutes, then add ¼ cup (60 ml) of water. Season with salt and pepper. Simmer the artichokes gently until tender, stirring often and adding more water as required.

5. Cook the fettuccine in a large pot of salted boiling water until al dente, 3–4 minutes.

6. Drain well and add to the pan with the artichokes. Sprinkle with the parsley and pecorino, toss well, and serve hot.

AMOUNT PER SERVING	534	20g	28g	2g	54g	0.7g
NUTRITION FACTS	CALORIES	PROTEIN	FAT	FIBER	CARBS	SALT
PERCENT DAILY VALUES (based on 2000 calories)	26%	43%	35%	8%	42%	12%

If you liked this recipe, you will love these as well.

whole-wheat penne with tuna, avocado & fresh herbs
180

pasta with goat cheese & artichokes
168

bucatini with eggs & artichokes
276

fettuccine with creamy eggplant sauce

The best eggplants are firm and shiny with unbroken skin. Freshness is important, so don't store them for very long. If you don't have time to make the pasta at home, use 14 ounces (400 g) of ordinary fettuccine.

Serves 4

30 minutes

Time for pasta

25 minutes

2

PASTA

14	ounces (400 g) fresh fettuccine (see pages 16–25)
2	dried chiles, crumbled
1	teaspoon finely chopped fresh thyme

SAUCE

3	medium eggplant (aubergines), peeled and chopped into small cubes
⅓	cup (90 ml) extra-virgin olive oil
2	cloves garlic, finely chopped
1	tablespoon finely chopped fresh thyme
15	leaves fresh basil, torn
	Salt
3	tomatoes, chopped
6	tablespoons freshly grated aged pecorino cheese

1. **Prepare the fettuccine** following the instructions on pages 16–25, adding the chile and thyme to the egg yolks.

2. **To prepare the sauce,** boil the eggplant in lightly salted water for 4 minutes. Drain, squeezing out any excess moisture.

3. **Heat** the oil in a large frying pan over medium heat. Add the garlic and thyme and sauté for 2 minutes. Add the eggplant and cook for 6–7 minutes, mashing gently with a fork. Remove from the heat, add half the basil, and season with salt.

4. **Transfer** to a food processor and chop until smooth. Return the eggplant cream to the pan and add the tomatoes. Cook until the tomatoes have broken down and the sauce is creamy.

5. **Cook** the pasta in a large pot of salted boiling water until al dente, 3–4 minutes.

6. **Drain well,** reserving 2–3 tablespoons of the cooking water. Add to the pan with the reserved water, sprinkle with the cheese and remaining basil, and toss gently. Serve hot.

AMOUNT PER SERVING	710	24g	33g	8g	84g	0.5g
NUTRITION FACTS	**CALORIES**	**PROTEIN**	**FAT**	**FIBER**	**CARBS**	**SALT**
PERCENT DAILY VALUES (based on 2000 calories)	34%	52%	41%	32%	65%	10%

If you liked this recipe, you will love these as well.

pasta salad with eggplant & pine nuts
122

penne with bell peppers, eggplant & zucchini
126

spaghetti with fried eggplant & tomato
280

fettuccine with spicy chicken sauce

This is a hearty dish that can be served as a meal in itself.

 Serves 4

 30 minutes

Time for pasta

 40 minutes

2

14	ounces (400 g) fresh , homemade fettuccine (see pages 16–25), or store-bought
2	boneless, skinless chicken breast halves, thinly sliced
1	tablespoon spicy paprika
1	tablespoon curry powder
	Salt
¼	cup (60 ml) extra-virgin olive oil
1	carrot, finely chopped
1	stalk celery, finely chopped
1	onion, finely chopped
½	cup (125 ml) dry white wine
1	pound (500 g) tomatoes, peeled and chopped
¼	cup (60 ml) vegetable stock
2	tablespoons freshly squeezed lemon juice
	Freshly ground black pepper
2	tablespoons fresh basil

1. If using homemade pasta, prepare the fettuccine following the instructions on pages 16–25.

2. To prepare the sauce, put the chicken in a large bowl and dust with the paprika, curry powder, and salt.

3. Heat the oil in a large frying pan over medium heat. Add the carrot, celery, and onion and sauté until the onion is transparent, 3–4 minutes.

4. Add the chicken and sauté until browned all over, 5–7 minutes.

Add the wine and let it evaporate. Add the tomatoes and mix well.

5. Cover and simmer over low heat for 25 minutes, adding a little stock if the sauce dries out. Stir in the lemon juice and season with salt and pepper.

6. Cook the pasta in a large pot of salted boiling water until al dente, 4–5 minutes. Drain, reserving 2 tablespoons of cooking liquid. Toss with the sauce over high heat for 1 minute. Add the reserved cooking liquid and toss again. Sprinkle with basil and serve hot.

AMOUNT PER SERVING	622	28g	22g	5g	78g	0.5g
NUTRITION FACTS	CALORIES	PROTEIN	FAT	FIBER	CARBS	SALT
PERCENT DAILY VALUES (based on 2000 calories)	30%	61%	27%	20%	60%	10%

If you liked this recipe, you will love these as well.

penne with spicy tomato sauce

160

baked spaghetti with chicken & spinach

314

pappardelle with pumpkin & saffron

Not only is pumpkin delicious, but it is also very good for you! It is a rich source of fiber, vitamin A, beta-carotene, potassium, and selenium.

- Serves 4
- 30 minutes
- Time for pasta
- 50 minutes

- 2

14	ounces (400 g) fresh pappardelle, homemade (see pages 16–25), or store-bought
3	small leeks, sliced
1/3	cup (90 ml) extra-virgin olive oil
1/2	cup (125 ml) light (single) cream
1/4	cup (30 g) freshly grated Parmesan cheese
1/4	cup (60 ml) vegetable stock
	Pinch of curry powder

	Salt and freshly ground black pepper
8	ounces (250 g) fresh pumpkin, or winter squash, peeled, seeded, and cubed
1/2	tablespoon finely chopped fresh thyme
1/2	tablespoon finely chopped fresh marjoram
1/4	cup (45 g) pine nuts
1	tablespoon butter
1	shallot, thinly sliced
	Pinch of saffron strands

1. If using homemade pasta, prepare the pappardelle following the instructions on pages 16–25.

2. Preheat the oven to 375°F (190°C/gas 5). Blanch the leeks in salted boiling water until tender, 4–5 minutes. Drain and transfer to a food processor. Add 3 tablespoons of oil, the cream, Parmesan, stock, curry powder, salt, and pepper and chop until smooth.

4. Put the pumpkin on an oiled baking sheet. Drizzle with the remaining oil and season with salt and pepper. Top with the thyme, marjoram, and pine nuts and bake until tender, 12–15 minutes.

5. Melt the butter in a large frying pan over medium heat. Add the shallot and sauté until tender, 3–4 minutes. Add the pumpkin and leek purée. Mix well.

6. Cook the pasta in a large pot of salted boiling water with the saffron until al dente, 3–4 minutes. Drain and add to the sauce. Toss over high heat for 1 minute. Serve hot.

AMOUNT PER SERVING NUTRITION FACTS PERCENT DAILY VALUES (based on 2 000 calories)	860 CALORIES 41%	24g PROTEIN 52%	48g FAT 59%	6g FIBER 24%	84g CARBS 65%	0.7g SALT 12%

If you liked this recipe, you will love these as well.

ravioli with pumpkin sauce

94

lasagna with pumpkin

110

fresh pasta with beans

If you can't find fresh cranberry (borlotti) beans, you can use canned. Buy two 14-ounce (400-g) cans and add the beans at step 4. You can also replace the beans with red kidney or pinto beans.

Serves 4

30 minutes

Time for pasta

1 hour 30 minutes

2

BEANS & PASTA

14 ounces (400 g) fresh shelled red kidney beans
8   cups (2 liters) cold water
2   cloves garlic
1   bunch fresh sage
2   tablespoons extra-virgin olive oil
    Salt
14 ounces (400 g) fresh homemade pasta dough (see pages 16–25)

SAUCE

2   tablespoons extra-virgin olive oil
2   cloves garlic, finely chopped
2   tablespoons finely chopped fresh parsley
6   firm-ripe tomatoes, coarsely chopped
    Salt and freshly ground black pepper

1. **Put the beans** in a large saucepan with the water, garlic, sage, and oil. Bring to a boil and simmer over low heat until the beans are tender, about 1 hour. Season with salt and drain, reserving a little of the cooking water.

2. **Prepare the pasta dough** following the instructions on pages 16–25.

3. **To prepare the sauce,** heat the oil in a frying pan over medium heat, add the garlic and parsley, and sauté until the garlic is pale gold, 2–3 minutes.

4. **Stir in** the tomatoes and season with salt. Simmer over medium-low heat for 20 minutes. Add the beans and a few tablespoons of their cooking water.

5. **Roll** the dough out on a lightly floured work surface into a thin sheet. Cut into irregularly shaped pieces.

6. **Cook** the pasta in a large pot of salted boiling water until al dente, 3–4 minutes. Drain well and serve hot with the bean sauce and plenty of pepper.

AMOUNT PER SERVING NUTRITION FACTS PERCENT DAILY VALUES (based on 2000 calories)	632 CALORIES 30%	24g PROTEIN 52%	19g FAT 23%	10g FIBER 40%	97g CARBS 75%	1.1g SALT 21%

If you liked this recipe, you will love these as well.

spirals with beans & pesto

150

spaghetti with chili

304

whole-wheat spaghetti
with spicy tomato sauce

Homemade spaghetti is thick and delicious. It soaks up the sauce. You can buy a *chitarra* (a "guitar" in Italian, named for its shape) in specialty kitchen supply stores to cut the pasta sheets into spaghetti. Otherwise use a sharp knife and a steady hand.

Serves 4

45 minutes

1 hour

15 minutes

 3

PASTA DOUGH

2¹⁄₃ cups (350 g) whole-wheat (wholemeal) flour

¹⁄₄ teaspoon salt
Lukewarm water

SAUCE

¹⁄₃ cup (90 ml) extra-virgin olive oil

2 cloves garlic, finely chopped

1 fresh red chile, finely chopped

1 tablespoon finely chopped fresh parsley

1¹⁄₄ pounds (750 g) tomatoes, peeled and chopped
Salt

1. **To prepare the pasta dough,** mound the flour and salt up on a clean work surface and make a well in the center. Mix in enough water to make a smooth dough. Knead until smooth and elastic, 10–15 minutes. Shape into a ball, wrap in plastic wrap (cling film), and let rest for 30 minutes.

2. **Roll out** the dough on a lightly floured work surface until about ¹⁄₈ inch (3 mm) thick. Cover with a cloth and let dry for 30 minutes.

3. **To prepare the sauce,** heat the oil in a large frying pan over medium heat. Add the garlic, chile, and parsley and sauté until the garlic is gold, 2–3 minutes.

4. **Stir in** the tomatoes and cook over high heat until the tomatoes have broken down, about 5 minutes. Season with salt.

5. **Cut** the pasta into spaghetti using a chitarra. If you don't have a chitarra, use a sharp knife to cut the pasta into ¹⁄₈-inch (3-mm) strips.

6. **Cook** the pasta in a large pot of salted boiling water until al dente, 2–3 minutes.

7. **Drain well** and add to the sauce. Toss gently over medium heat until the sauce sticks to the pasta. Serve hot.

AMOUNT PER SERVING	486 CALORIES	13g PROTEIN	23g FAT	10g FIBER	62g CARBS	0.5g SALT
NUTRITION FACTS						
PERCENT DAILY VALUES (based on 2000 calories)	23%	28%	28%	40%	48%	9%

If you liked this recipe, you will love these as well.

fettuccine with roasted tomato sauce

40

penne with spicy tomato sauce

160

cool fusilli with tomatoes & onion

120

homemade spaghetti
with garlic & oil

Extra-virgin olive oil contains heart-healthy monounsaturated fat. It is fairly high in calories, so 2–3 tablespoons each day is plenty. Fresh parsley and garlic make this dish super-healthy!

Serves 4

30 minutes

1 hour 30 minutes

5 minutes

2

PASTA DOUGH

2⅓ cups (350 g) all-purpose (plain) flour

¼ teaspoon salt

Lukewarm water

SAUCE

5 tablespoons (75 ml) extra-virgin olive oil

6 cloves garlic, finely chopped

6 tablespoons finely chopped fresh parsley

1. **To prepare the pasta dough,** mound the flour and salt up on a wooden work surface and make a well in the center. Add enough water to make a firm dough. Knead until smooth and elastic, 15–20 minutes. Set aside for 30 minutes.

2. **Break off** pieces of dough and roll them into thick spaghetti about 8 inches (20 cm) long. Leave to dry covered with a cloth for at least 1 hour.

3. **Cook** the pasta in a large pot of salted boiling water until al dente, 3–4 minutes. Drain well and place in a heated serving bowl.

4. **Heat** the oil with the garlic in a small saucepan over low heat until the garlic is pale gold, 3–4 minutes.

5. **Drizzle** the garlic and oil over the pasta and sprinkle with parsley. Toss gently and serve hot.

AMOUNT PER SERVING	450	8g	18g	3g	68g	0.5g
NUTRITION FACTS	**CALORIES**	**PROTEIN**	**FAT**	**FIBER**	**CARBS**	**SALT**
PERCENT DAILY VALUES (based on 2000 calories)	22%	17%	22%	12%	52%	9%

If you liked this recipe, you will love these as well.

homemade spaghetti with tomato & garlic sauce

56

spaghetti with lemon & olives

232

spaghetti with garlic, chile & oil

224

homemade spaghetti
with tomato & garlic sauce

The secret for success with this old Tuscan recipe is to simmer the tomatoes over very low heat until the garlic has almost dissolved. Vary the amount of red pepper flakes to taste.

Serves 4

45 minutes

1 hour 30 minutes

1 hour

3

PASTA DOUGH

2⅓ cups (350 g) all-purpose (plain) flour
¼ teaspoon salt
    Lukewarm water

SAUCE

5   tablespoons extra-virgin olive oil
10 cloves garlic, lightly crushed, but whole
2   pounds (1 kg) tomatoes, peeled and finely chopped
¼   teaspoon dried red pepper flakes
    Salt

1. **To prepare the pasta dough,** mound the flour and salt up on a wooden work surface and make a well in the center. Add enough water to make a firm dough. Knead until smooth and elastic, 15–20 minutes. Set aside for 30 minutes.

2. **Break off** pieces of dough and roll them into thick spaghetti about 8 inches (20 cm) long. Leave to dry covered with a cloth for at least 1 hour.

3. **To prepare the garlic sauce,** pour the oil into a large frying pan over medium heat. Add the garlic and sauté until pale gold, 3–4 minutes.

4. **Add** the tomatoes and red pepper flakes and season with salt. Partially cover the pan and simmer over low heat until the garlic has almost dissolved into the sauce, about 45 minutes. Season with salt.

5. **Cook** the pasta in a large pot of salted boiling water until al dente, 3–4 minutes.

6. **Drain well** and place in a heated serving bowl. Add the sauce, tossing gently. Serve hot.

AMOUNT PER SERVING	460	11g	15g	6g	75g	0.5g
NUTRITION FACTS	CALORIES	PROTEIN	FAT	FIBER	CARBS	SALT
PERCENT DAILY VALUES (based on 2000 calories)	22%	24%	19%	24%	58%	9%

If you liked this recipe, you will love these as well.

homemade spaghetti with garlic & oil
54

penne with spicy tomato sauce
160

spaghetti with garlic, chile & oil
224

homemade spaghetti
with tomatoes & arugula

If you can't find arugula, use baby spinach leaves, which work just as well, although they have a slightly milder flavor.

Serves 4

40 minutes

1 hour 30 minutes

30 minutes

2

PASTA DOUGH

2⅓ cups (350 g) all-purpose (plain) flour

¼ teaspoon salt

Lukewarm water

SAUCE

5 tablespoons extra-virgin olive oil

2 cloves garlic, finely chopped

1 dried chile, crumbled

2 cups (500 ml) peeled and chopped tomatoes

1 bunch arugula (rocket), shredded

1 stalk celery, chopped

½ cup (60 g) Parmesan cheese, in flakes

1 tablespoon finely chopped fresh parsley

1. To prepare the pasta dough, mound the flour and salt up on a wooden work surface and make a well in the center. Add enough water to make a firm dough. Knead until smooth and elastic, 15–20 minutes. Set aside for 30 minutes.

2. Break off pieces of dough and roll them into thick spaghetti about 8 inches (20 cm) long. Leave to dry covered with a cloth for 1 hour.

3. To prepare the sauce, heat the oil in a large frying pan over medium heat.

Add the garlic and chile and sauté until the garlic is pale gold, 3–4 minutes. Stir in the tomatoes and simmer for 15 minutes over medium-low heat.

4. Cook the pasta in a large pot of salted boiling water until al dente, 3–4 minutes.

5. Drain well and add to the sauce. Add the arugula, celery, Parmesan, and parsley. Toss well and serve hot.

AMOUNT PER SERVING	530 CALORIES	15g PROTEIN	23g FAT	4g FIBER	73g CARBS	0.4g SALT
NUTRITION FACTS PERCENT DAILY VALUES (based on 2000 calories)	25%	33%	28%	16%	56%	7%

If you liked this recipe, you will love these as well.

fusilli salad with bell peppers & arugula

116

whole-wheat spaghetti with summer vegetables

256

fettuccine with scallops

Scallops are a good source of vitamin B12, omega-3 fatty acids, and magnesium, all of which promote good cardiovascular health. Use more or less chiles according to taste.

 Serves 4

 10 minutes

Time for pasta

20 minutes

2

14	ounces (400 g) fresh fettuccine, homemade (see pages 16–25), or store-bought
12	large scallops, with corals
½	cup (125 ml) extra-virgin olive oil
½	cup (60 g) fine dry bread crumbs

4	tablespoons finely chopped fresh parsley
2	cloves garlic, finely chopped
½	teaspoon crushed dried chiles or red pepper flakes
	Salt
¼	cup (60 ml) dry white wine

1. **If using homemade pasta,** prepare the fettuccine following the instructions on pages 16–25.

2. **Detach** the corals from the scallops and set aside. Slice each white scallop into 3 or 4 pieces.

3. **Heat** 2 tablespoons of oil in a medium frying pan over medium heat. Add the bread crumbs and sauté until golden, 3–5 minutes. Transfer to a small bowl and set aside.

3. **Heat** 5 tablespoons of the remaining oil in the same frying pan over medium heat. Add 2 tablespoons of parsley, the garlic, and chiles and sauté until their flavors are released, 2–3 minutes.

4. **Meanwhile,** cook the fettuccine in a large pot of salted boiling water until al dente, 3–4 minutes. Drain well, return to the pot, and toss with the remaining 1 tablespoon of oil.

5. **Stir** the white parts of the scallops into the frying pan and sauté until they start to turn opaque, about 30 seconds. Add the wine and reserved scallop corals, simmer for 30 seconds, then add the fettuccine and cook for 1 minute, tossing to combine.

7. **Sprinkle** with the bread crumbs and the remaining parsley and serve hot.

AMOUNT PER SERVING	609 CALORIES	21g PROTEIN	30g FAT	3g FIBER	67g CARBS	0.3g SALT
NUTRITION FACTS PERCENT DAILY VALUES (based on 2 000 calories)	29%	46%	37%	12%	52%	5%

If you liked this recipe, you will love these as well.

cavatappi with shrimp & asparagus

172

penne with tomato & shrimp

186

spaghetti with seafood

298

fettuccine with mussels

Use well-ripened, fresh red tomatoes for best results with this recipe. Buy fresh mussels, too; if necessary remove from their shells by steaming them open, then removing the mollusks.

Serves 4

20 minutes

Time for pasta

30 minutes

2

14	ounces (400 g) fresh fettuccine, homemade (see pages 16–25), or store-bought
1 ½	pounds (750 g) tomatoes
1	tablespoon extra-virgin olive oil
1	onion, finely chopped
2	cloves garlic, finely chopped
2	stalks celery, finely chopped
1	red bell pepper (capsicum), finely chopped

4	ounces (125 g) button mushrooms, thinly sliced
4	sun-dried tomatoes, soaked, drained, and finely chopped
½	cup (125 ml) dry red wine
2	tablespoons tomato purée
	Salt and freshly ground black pepper
8	ounces (250 g) mussels
2	tablespoons finely chopped fresh basil

1. If using homemade pasta, prepare the fettuccine following the instructions on pages 16–25.

2. To prepare the sauce, cover the tomatoes with boiling water and leave for 30 seconds. Drain, peel, and seed, then chop the flesh.

3. Heat the oil in a large saucepan over medium heat. Add the onion, garlic, celery, bell pepper, and mushrooms, and sauté until softened, 4–5 minutes.

4. Mix in the fresh and dried tomatoes, red wine, and tomato purée. Season with salt and pepper. Bring to a boil, cover, then simmer over low heat until tender, about 20 minutes.

5. Stir in the mussels. Increase the heat slightly and cook, uncovered, for 5 minutes, stirring occasionally.

6. Cook the fettuccine in a large pot of salted boiling water until al dente, 3–4 minutes. Drain, add to the sauce with the basil, and toss well. Serve hot.

AMOUNT PER SERVING	648	27g	19g	7g	92g	1g
NUTRITION FACTS	CALORIES	PROTEIN	FAT	FIBER	CARBS	SALT
PERCENT DAILY VALUES (based on 2 000 calories)	31%	59%	23%	28%	71%	19%

If you liked this recipe, you will love these as well.

penne with mussels

190

seafood spaghetti en papillote

302

spaghetti with mussels

294

fettuccine with salmon & peas

If desired, use fresh salmon instead of smoked. Poach 14 ounces (400 g) of salmon fillets in some finely chopped fresh mixed herbs and a little milk until cooked, then break into chunks with a fork. Add to the sauce at step 4.

Serves 4

10 minutes

Time for pasta

10 minutes

2

14 ounces (400 g) fresh fettuccine, homemade (see pages 16–25), or store-bought

1 cup (150 g) frozen peas

½ cup (60 ml) dry white wine

1¼ cups (300 ml) light (single) cream

8 large slices smoked salmon

3 scallions (spring onions), finely chopped

Salt and freshly ground black pepper

1. **If using homemade pasta,** prepare the fettuccine following the instructions on pages 16–25.

2. **To prepare the sauce,** blanch the peas in boiling water for 2 minutes. Refresh under cold running water, drain, and set aside.

3. **Pour** the wine into a large frying pan and bring to a boil. Stir in 1 cup (250 ml) of cream and boil until the sauce reduces and thickens.

4. **Combine** 4 slices of smoked salmon, the scallions, and remaining cream in a food processor and chop until smooth. Stir the smoked salmon mixture into the sauce and simmer until hot.

5. **Cook** the fettuccine in a large pot of salted boiling water until al dente, 3–4 minutes.

6. **Cut** the remaining salmon into thin strips. Add the salmon strips and peas to the sauce and season with salt and pepper.

7. **Drain** the pasta and put in a large bowl. Spoon the sauce over the top and toss to combine. Serve hot.

AMOUNT PER SERVING	717	41g	26g	6g	84g	1.9g
NUTRITION FACTS	CALORIES	PROTEIN	FAT	FIBER	CARBS	SALT
PERCENT DAILY VALUES (based on 2000 calories)	34%	89%	32%	24%	65%	34%

If you liked this recipe, you will love these as well.

salmon ravioli with lemon & dill

92

penne with smoked salmon

174

spaghetti with vodka & caviar

300

pappardelle marinara

You can buy ready-prepared bags of mixed seafood. Look for shrimp and mussels as well as bass, monkfish, haddock, and salmon. Avoid any smoked fish, such as smoked haddock.

 Serves 4

15 minutes

Time for pasta

10 minutes

2

14	ounces (400 g) fresh pappardelle, homemade (see pages 16–25), or store-bought
⅓	cup (90 ml) extra-virgin olive oil
1	onion, finely chopped
2	garlic cloves, finely chopped
⅔	cup (150 ml) dry white wine
½	cup (125 ml) fish stock or clam juice

2	cups (500 ml) tomato pasta sauce (see page 52)
3	tablespoons tomato paste
2	pounds (1 kg) mixed fresh seafood (shrimp, fish fillets, shelled mussels)
	Salt and freshly ground black pepper
⅓	cup (10 g) coarsely chopped fresh parsley

1. If using homemade pasta, prepare the pappardelle following the instructions on pages 16–25.

2. To prepare the sauce, heat the oil in a large frying pan over medium-high heat. Sauté the onion and garlic until softened, about 3 minutes.

3. Add the wine and simmer for 1 minute. Stir in the stock, tomato sauce, and tomato paste and bring to a boil, stirring from time to time.

4. Add the mixed seafood, cover, and simmer until the seafood is cooked through, 3–5 minutes. Season with salt and pepper.

5. Cook the pasta in a large pot of salted boiling water until al dente, 3–4 minutes.

6. Drain the pasta and return to the pan. Add the marinara sauce and parsley. Toss until well combined. Serve hot.

AMOUNT PER SERVING	1066	60g	52g	5g	87g	1.3g
NUTRITION FACTS	CALORIES	PROTEIN	FAT	FIBER	CARBS	SALT
PERCENT DAILY VALUES (based on 2 000 calories)	51%	130%	64%	20%	67%	24%

If you liked this recipe, you will love these as well.

spaghetti with seafood

184

penne with swordfish & salmon

188

seafood spaghetti en papillote

302

pappardelle with sausage & mushrooms

Fresh porcini are available only in late summer and fall, but you can always use the dried variety. Only a small amount of dried porcini is needed to add an intense flavor.

- Serves 4
- 30 minutes
- Time for pasta
- 50 minutes

2

14	ounces (400 g) fresh pappardelle, homemade (see pages 16–25), or store-bought
2	tablespoons extra-virgin olive oil
1	tablespoon butter
1	onion, finely chopped
12	ounces (350 g) Italian pork sausages, skinned and crumbled
1	ounce (30 g) dried porcini mushrooms, soaked in warm water for 10 minutes, drained, and chopped
¼	cup (60 ml) dry white wine
2	cups (400 g) canned tomatoes, with juice
2	fresh sage leaves, finely chopped
	Salt and freshly ground black pepper
¼	cup (30 g) freshly grated Parmesan cheese

1. If using homemade pasta, prepare the pappardelle following the instructions on pages 16–25.

2. Heat the oil and butter in a large frying pan over medium heat. Add the onion and sauté until softened, about 3 minutes.

3. Add the sausage and sauté until browned all over, about 5 minutes. Add the mushrooms and wine and cook until the wine has evaporated.

Add the tomatoes and simmer over low heat until the sauce is thick, about 20 minutes. Add the sage and season with salt and pepper.

4. Cook the pasta in a large pot of salted boiling water until al dente, 3–4 minutes.

5. Drain well and add to the pan with the sauce. Sauté for 1 minute over high heat. Sprinkle with the Parmesan and serve hot.

AMOUNT PER SERVING **NUTRITION FACTS** PERCENT DAILY VALUES (based on 2 000 calories)	897 CALORIES 43%	30g PROTEIN 65%	46g FAT 57%	4g FIBER 16%	94g CARBS 72%	2.1g SALT 38%

If you liked this recipe, you will love these as well.

festonati with italian sausages & broccoli

196

garganelli with creamy sausage sauce

202

fettuccine with meatballs

You can vary this dish by replacing half the ground beef with ground pork. For a spicier flavor, add a pinch of ground chile with the garlic and sage at step 5.

Serves 4

30 minutes

Time for pasta

50 minutes

2

14	ounces (400 g) fresh fettuccine, homemade (see pages 16–25), or store-bought
2	small zucchini (courgettes), sliced thinly
1	pound (500 g) ripe tomatoes
1/4	cup (60 ml) extra-virgin olive oil
2	scallions (spring onions), white part and green part sliced separately
2	cloves garlic, finely chopped
4	sage leaves, finely chopped

1	tablespoon finely chopped fresh rosemary
	Salt
12	ounces (350 g) lean ground (minced) beef
1	large egg, lightly beaten
2	cups (120 g) fresh bread crumbs
2	tablespoons finely chopped fresh basil
2	tablespoons finely chopped fresh parsley
	Freshly ground black pepper

1. **If using homemade pasta**, prepare the fettuccine following the instructions on pages 16–25.

2. **Cook** the zucchini in a pot of salted boiling water until tender, 3–5 minutes. Remove from the heat and drain, reserving the cooking liquid.

3. **Blanch** the tomatoes in boiling water for 2 minutes. Drain well, slip off the skins, and chop the flesh.

4. **Heat** 2 tablespoons of oil in a large frying pan over medium heat. Add the white part of the scallions and sauté until softened, about 3 minutes.

5. **Add** the garlic, sage, rosemary, and tomatoes. Season with salt. Simmer over low heat until the tomatoes have broken down, about 10 minutes. Add the zucchini. Simmer until tender, about 10 minutes. Remove from the heat.

6. **Mix** the beef, egg, half the bread crumbs, green part of the scallions, basil, and parsley in a large bowl. Season with salt and pepper. Shape the meat mixture into balls about the size of a small walnut. Roll in the remaining bread crumbs.

7. **Heat** the remaining oil in a large frying pan over medium-high heat. Add the meatballs and sauté until cooked through and lightly browned, 8–10 minutes. Remove using a slotted spoon. Drain on paper towels.

8. **Return** the reserved cooking liquid from the zucchini to a large saucepan and bring to a boil. Add the pasta and cook for 3–4 minutes, or until al dente. Drain well. Transfer to the frying pan with the sauce and toss over a high heat for 1 minute. Add the meatballs and mix well. Serve hot.

AMOUNT PER SERVING						
NUTRITION FACTS PERCENT DAILY VALUES (based on 2000 calories)	768 CALORIES 37%	35g PROTEIN 76%	34g FAT 42%	5g FIBER 20%	86g CARBS 66%	0.7g SALT 12%

pappardelle with duck ragù

If you don't want to buy a whole duck, you can use ready-prepared breasts. Make sure you remove the skin before cooking. If preparing a whole duck, use the carcass to make stock.

 Serves 6

⏱ 30 minutes

🔥 Time for pasta

⏲ 2 hours

🍴 2

14	ounces (400 g) fresh pappardelle, homemade (see pages 16–25), or store-bought
5	tablespoons extra-virgin olive oil
1	red onion, finely chopped
1	bay leaf
4	sage leaves, finely chopped
½	carrot, finely chopped
1	tablespoon finely chopped fresh parsley
2	celery leaves, finely chopped
3	ounces (90 g) ham, chopped
1	duck (about 3 pounds/ 1.5 kg), cleaned and cut in 4 pieces
⅔	cup (150 ml) dry red wine
2	cups (400 g) canned tomatoes, with juice
	Salt and freshly ground black pepper
¾	cup (180 ml) beef stock (homemade or from bouillon cube)
½	cup (60 g) freshly grated Parmesan cheese

1. **If using homemade pasta,** prepare the pappardelle following the instructions on pages 16–25.

2. **Heat** the oil in a large saucepan over low heat. Sauté the onion, bay leaf, sage, carrot, parsley, celery leaves, and ham for 15 minutes.

3. **Add** the duck and sauté over high heat until well browned, about 10 minutes. Pour in the wine and simmer for 15 more minutes.

4. **Stir in** the tomatoes and season with salt and pepper. Pour in the stock, cover, and simmer for 1 hour.

5. **Bone** the duck and cut the meat into small chunks. Return the meat to the sauce and simmer for 15 minutes.

6. **Cook** the pasta in a large pot of salted boiling water until al dente, 3–4 minutes. Drain and add to the sauce. Sprinkle with the Parmesan, toss well, and serve hot.

AMOUNT PER SERVING	624	44g	24g	3g	56g	1.4g
NUTRITION FACTS	CALORIES	PROTEIN	FAT	FIBER	CARBS	SALT
PERCENT DAILY VALUES (based on 2000 calories)	30%	96%	30%	12%	43%	26%

If you liked this recipe, you will love these as well.

pappardelle with duck sauce
74

fettuccine roman style
76

pappardelle with meat sauce
78

pappardelle with duck sauce

This simple recipe looks and tastes very special, yet is ready in minutes. You can replace the duck with turkey or chicken.

 Serves 6

 15 minutes

Time for pasta

15 minutes

2

14	ounces (400 g) fresh pappardelle, homemade (see pages 16–25), or storebought
1½	pounds (750 g) duck breasts
2	tablespoons extra-virgin olive oil
1	onion, diced
2	cloves garlic, crushed
14	ounces (400 g) tomatoes, peeled and coarsely chopped
⅔	cup (150 ml) chicken stock
	Salt and freshly ground black pepper
1½	cups (150 g) black olives
10	fresh sage leaves

1. If using homemade pasta, prepare the pappardelle following the instructions on pages 16–25.

2. To prepare the sauce, put the duck breasts in a medium saucepan, cover with water, and boil for 5 minutes. Strain the water, and remove the skin from the breasts. Cut the meat into strips and set aside.

3. Heat the oil in a large frying pan over medium heat. Add the onion and garlic and sauté until softened, about 3 minutes.

4. Add the duck pieces and sauté for 1 minute. Add the tomatoes and stock and simmer until the sauce thickens, 5–10 minutes.

5. Cook the pasta in a large pot of salted boiling water until al dente, 3–4 minutes.

6. Drain the pasta and add to the pan with the sauce. Season with salt and pepper, add the olives and sage, and toss well. Serve hot.

AMOUNT PER SERVING	532	40g	18g	3g	56g	0.8g
NUTRITION FACTS	CALORIES	PROTEIN	FAT	FIBER	CARBS	SALT
PERCENT DAILY VALUES (based on 2000 calories)	26%	87%	22%	12%	43%	15%

If you liked this recipe, you will love these as well.

pappardelle with duck ragù

72

fettuccine roman style

76

pappardelle with meat sauce

78

fettuccine roman style

This classic Roman sauce also goes very well with spinach or whole-wheat fettuccine. Serve with a glass of dry red wine.

 Serves 4

 30 minutes

 Time for pasta

 1 hour 40 minutes

 2

14	ounces (400 g) fresh fettuccine, homemade (see pages 16–25), or store-bought
¼	cup (60 ml) extra-virgin olive oil
1	red onion, finely chopped
1	small carrot, finely chopped
1	stalk celery, finely chopped
12	ounces (350 g) lean ground (minced) beef
⅓	cup (90 ml) dry red wine
4	ounces (125 g) chicken livers, trimmed and diced

2	cups (400 g) canned tomatoes, with juice
½	ounce (15 g) dried porcini mushrooms, soaked in warm water for 10 minutes and finely chopped
1	bay leaf
	Salt and freshly ground black pepper
¾	cup (75 g) freshly grated Parmesan cheese
2	tablespoons butter, diced

1. **If using homemade pasta,** prepare the fettuccine following the instructions on pages 16–25.

2. **Heat** the oil in a large saucepan over medium heat. Add the onion, carrot, and celery and sauté until the onion is lightly browned, about 5 minutes.

3. **Stir in** the beef and sauté until browned all over, 5–7 minutes. Pour in the wine and cook until evaporated, about 4 minutes.

4. **Add** the chicken livers and simmer over low heat for 15 minutes.

5. **Add** the tomatoes, mushrooms, and bay leaf and season with salt and pepper. Cover and simmer over low heat for 1 hour. Remove the bay leaf.

6. **Cook** the pasta in a large pot of salted boiling water until al dente, 3–4 minutes. Drain and add to the sauce. Top with the Parmesan and butter. Toss well and serve hot.

AMOUNT PER SERVING NUTRITION FACTS PERCENT DAILY VALUES (based on 2,000 calories)	1000 CALORIES 50%	44g PROTEIN 96%	49g FAT 60%	5g FIBER 20%	91g CARBS 70%	1g SALT 17%

If you liked this recipe, you will love these as well.

pappardelle with duck ragù

72

pappardelle with duck sauce

74

pappardelle with meat sauce

78

pappardelle with meat sauce

This wonderful dish takes some time to cook but is well worth the effort. Follow with a mixed salad for a healthy and delicious family meal.

Serves 4

20 minutes

Time for pasta

2 hours 45 minutes

2

14 ounces (400 g) fresh pappardelle, homemade (see pages 16–25), or store-bought

3 tablespoons extra-virgin olive oil

2 tablespoons butter

4 ounces (125 g) pancetta, coarsely chopped

1 small onion, finely chopped

1 small carrot, finely chopped

1 stalk celery, finely chopped

1 clove garlic, finely chopped

1 pound (500 g) ground (minced) beef

½ cup (125 ml) dry white wine

2 tablespoons tomato paste (concentrate)

½ cup (125 ml) beef stock
Salt and freshly ground black pepper

½ cup (125 ml) milk
Freshly grated Parmesan cheese

1. **If using homemade pasta,** prepare the pappardelle following the instructions on pages 16–25.

2. **Heat** the oil and butter in a large saucepan over medium heat. Add the pancetta, onion, carrot, celery, and garlic and sauté until the vegetables have softened, about 5 minutes.

3. **Add** the beef and sauté until browned, about 5 minutes. Pour in the wine and simmer for 2–3 minutes, until reduced by more than half.

4. **Mix in** the tomato paste, stock, and seasoning. Return to a boil, then simmer very gently, uncovered, for about 2 hours 30 minutes, stirring from time to time. Add 2 tablespoons of milk if the sauce starts to dry out.

5. **Cook** the pasta in a large pot of salted boiling water until al dente, 3–4 minutes.

6. **Drain** and transfer to a serving bowl. Add the sauce and toss well. Serve hot with the Parmesan cheese.

AMOUNT PER SERVING	925	49g	44g	4g	85g	1.8g
NUTRITION FACTS	CALORIES	PROTEIN	FAT	FIBER	CARBS	SALT
PERCENT DAILY VALUES (based on 2000 calories)	45%	107%	54%	16%	65%	33%

If you liked this recipe, you will love these as well.

fettuccine roman style

76

lasagna with meatballs

108

penne with meat sauce

208

saffron pappardelle
with lamb sauce

This is a classic recipe from Umbria, in central Italy. With its saffron-infused pasta and rich lamb sauce, it is perfect for a wintry Sunday lunch.

Serves 6

30 minutes

1 hour

1 hour 30 minutes

3

PASTA DOUGH

2¾ cups (500 g) all-purpose (plain) flour + extra for dusting

4 fresh large eggs + 2 fresh large egg yolks

1 teaspoon ground saffron, dissolved in 1 tablespoon warm water

SAUCE

¼ cup (60 ml) extra-virgin olive oil

3 tablespoons butter

1 leg of lamb, weighing about 2½ pounds (1.2 kg)

½ cup (125 ml) Vin Santo or sherry

Salt and freshly ground white pepper

4 cups (1 liter) beef stock

1 small onion, finely chopped

2 tablespoons all-purpose (plain) flour

1 lettuce heart, cut in strips

1 tablespoon finely chopped marjoram

6–8 threads saffron, crumbled

1. Prepare the pappardelle using the ingredients listed here and following the instructions on pages 16–23, adding the saffron and water mixture to the eggs.

2. To prepare the sauce, heat the oil and butter in a large saucepan over high heat and sauté the lamb until browned all over, 7–8 minutes.

3. Pour in the wine or sherry and cook until evaporated. Season with salt and white pepper, lower the heat, and simmer until very tender, at least 1 hour, adding enough stock to keep the sauce moist.

4. Remove the lamb from the pan and cut the meat from the bone. Cut into small strips.

5. Add 3 tablespoons of stock to the pan with the cooking juices. Add the onion and simmer for 5 minutes. Add the lamb and simmer for 5 minutes.

6. Stir in the flour and 2 cups (500 ml) of stock. Add the lettuce, marjoram, and saffron and season with salt and white pepper. Cook over low heat for about 5 minutes or until the lettuce has wilted and the sauce has thickened.

7. Meanwhile, cook the pasta in a large pot of salted boiling water until al dente, 3–4 minutes. Drain well and transfer to a heated serving dish. Spoon the sauce over the top and toss gently. Serve hot.

fettuccine with pancetta & radicchio

Red Treviso radicchio, also known as red chicory, has a lovely, slightly bitter flavor.

 Serves 4

Time for pasta

25 minutes

 1

14	ounces (400 g) fresh fettuccine, homemade (see pages 16–25), or store-bought
3	tablespoons butter
1	red onion, finely chopped
1	cup (125 g) pancetta, cut into thin slices
1	pound (500 g) red Treviso radicchio (or chicory), finely shredded
	Salt and freshly ground black pepper
1	cup (250 ml) dry red wine

1. **If using homemade pasta,** prepare the fettuccine following the instructions on pages 16–25.

2. **Melt** the butter in a large frying pan over medium heat. Add the onion and sauté until softened, 3–4 minutes.

3. **Add** the pancetta and sauté until crisp, about 5 minutes.

4. **Add** the radicchio and season with salt and pepper. Pour in the wine and simmer until it evaporates.

5. **Cook** the pasta in a large pot of salted boiling water until al dente, 3–4 minutes.

6. **Drain** and add to the pan with the radicchio. Toss carefully and serve hot.

AMOUNT PER SERVING	628	24g	20g	5g	84g	1.2g
NUTRITION FACTS	CALORIES	PROTEIN	FAT	FIBER	CARBS	SALT
PERCENT DAILY VALUES (based on 2000 calories)	30%	52%	25%	20%	65%	21%

If you liked this recipe, you will love these as well.

tortellini with pancetta & leeks
98

spaghetti with bell peppers & pancetta
260

bucatini with amatriciana sauce
272

orecchiette with broccoli

Orecchiette, literally "little ears" in Italian, come from the southern Puglia region. There it is traditional to cook the pasta in the same water that is used to cook the vegetables—a wonderful way of preserving precious vitamins.

Serves 4

5 minutes

40 minutes

1

14	ounces (400 g) broccoli
¼	cup (60 ml) extra-virgin olive oil
2	cloves garlic, finely chopped
1	fresh red chile, seeded and thinly sliced

	Salt
14	ounces (400 g) fresh or dried store-bought orecchiette
1¾	cups (200 g) freshly grated pecorino cheese

1. Trim the stem of the broccoli and dice into small cubes. Divide the broccoli head into small florets.

2. Boil the broccoli in a large saucepan of salted water until just tender, about 5 minutes. Drain well, reserving the water to cook the pasta.

3. Heat the oil in a large frying pan over medium heat. Add the garlic and sauté until pale golden brown, about 5 minutes. Add the broccoli and chile, season with salt. Simmer over low heat for 5 minutes. Remove from the heat.

4. Meanwhile, bring the water used to cook the broccoli back to a boil, add the pasta, and cook until al dente.

5. Drain well, and add to the broccoli sauce in the pan. Toss over high heat for 1–2 minutes. Sprinkle with the pecorino and serve hot.

AMOUNT PER SERVING	635	34g	32g	3g	58g	1g
NUTRITION FACTS	CALORIES	PROTEIN	FAT	FIBER	CARBS	SALT
PERCENT DAILY VALUES (based on 2000 calories)	31%	74%	40%	12%	45%	18%

If you liked this recipe, you will love these as well.

orecchiette with broccoli & pine nuts

88

festonati with italian sausages & broccoli

196

orecchiette with grilled bell pepper sauce

You can also prepare the bell peppers in the oven. Brush with a little oil and roast at the top of a 400°F (200°C/gas 6) oven until blackened all over, about 30 minutes.

 Serves 4

 20 minutes

30 minutes

 2

4 red bell peppers (capsicums)

14 ounces (400 g) fresh or dried store-bought orecchiette

1 cup (250 ml) light (single) cream

2 cups (100 g) baby spinach leaves, tough stems removed

¾ cup (180 g) feta cheese, cut into cubes

1. Broil (grill) the bell peppers until the skins are blackened all over. Wrap in a paper bag for 10 minutes, then remove the skins and seeds. Slice into strips.

2. Cook the orecchiette in a large saucepan of salted boiling water until al dente.

3. Transfer the bell peppers to a food processor. Chop until smooth, gradually pouring in the cream.

4. Pour the bell pepper sauce into a large frying pan and simmer over low heat for 3 minutes.

5. Drain the orecchiette and add to the pan with the sauce. Stir in the spinach and feta. Toss well and serve hot.

AMOUNT PER SERVING	526	22g	25g	3g	67g	1.7g
NUTRITION FACTS	CALORIES	PROTEIN	FAT	FIBER	CARBS	SALT
PERCENT DAILY VALUES (based on 2 000 calories)	25%	48%	31%	12%	52%	31%

If you liked this recipe, you will love these as well.

fusilli salad with bell peppers & arugula

116

baked penne with bell peppers

210

spaghetti with stuffed bell peppers

310

orecchiette with broccoli & pine nuts

Broccoli is a good source of beta-carotene. It also contains many plant compounds that are believed to be effective in preventing and fighting cancer.

 Serves 6

10 minutes

30 minutes

14 ounces (400 g) fresh or dried store-bought orecchiette
1 pound (500 g) broccoli
1 cup (250 ml) crème fraîche or sour cream

Pesto (see page 106)
¾ cup (135 g) pine nuts, toasted

1

1. **Cook** the orecchiette in a large saucepan of salted boiling water until al dente.

2. **Meanwhile,** boil the broccoli in a medium saucepan of boiling water for 5 minutes. Drain and rinse in ice-cold water to stop the cooking process.

3. **Mix** the crème fraîche and pesto in a large frying pan and over low heat for 2 minutes. Add the broccoli and pine nuts and simmer for 1 minute.

4. **Drain** the orecchiette and add to the pan with the sauce. Toss well and serve hot.

AMOUNT PER SERVING **NUTRITION FACTS** PERCENT DAILY VALUES (based on 2 000 calories)	666 CALORIES 32%	17g PROTEIN 37%	50g FAT 62%	3g FIBER 12%	41g CARBS 32%	1.4g SALT 26%

If you liked this recipe, you will love these as well.

fettuccine with pine nut & walnut pesto

38

orecchiette with broccoli

84

spaghetti with tomatoes, arugula & parmesan

252

ravioli with olive pesto

Olives, capers, and anchovies are three classic Italian ingredients, and they give this pasta dish an intense flavor and wonderful aroma.

Serves 6

10 minutes

20 minutes

1

½ cup (125 g) black olive paste

⅓ cup (90 ml) extra-virgin olive oil

14 ounces (400 g) store-bought ravioli, preferably with cheese or spinach filling

6 large ripe tomatoes, cut into small cubes

1 tablespoon salt-cured capers, rinsed

2 anchovy fillets preserved in oil, drained and finely chopped

10 leaves fresh basil, torn
Salt and freshly ground black pepper

1. Mix the olive paste with half the oil in a large bowl.

2. Cook the pasta in a large pot of salted boiling water until al dente.

3. Drain and add to the olive paste mixture, tossing gently. Drizzle with the remaining oil.

4. Add the tomatoes, capers, anchovies, and basil. Season with salt and pepper, then toss again. Serve at once.

AMOUNT PER SERVING NUTRITION FACTS PERCENT DAILY VALUES (based on 2 000 calories)	320 CALORIES 15%	9g PROTEIN 20%	21g FAT 26%	3g FIBER 12%	25g CARBS 19%	1.8g SALT 32%

If you liked this recipe, you will love these as well.

farfalle salad with cherry tomatoes & olives
114

pasta salad with eggplant & pine nuts
122

whole-wheat spaghetti with spicy sauce
266

salmon ravioli with lemon & dill

These delicately flavored ravioli make a delicious first course for an elegant dinner party. Serve with very cold, fruity dry white wine.

Serves 4

30 minutes

Time for pasta

10 minutes

3

RAVIOLI

14	ounces (400 g) fresh pasta dough (see pages 16–25)
4	ounces (125 g) smoked salmon pieces
1	egg white
1½	tablespoons light (single) cream
2	teaspoons fresh dill, coarsely chopped
3	tablespoons cornstarch (cornflour)
1	teaspoon oil

SAUCE

1	tablespoon butter
1	tablespoon all-purpose (plain) flour
¾	cup (180 ml) white wine
¾	cup (180 ml) heavy (double) cream
½	lemon, juiced
2	tablespoons coarsely chopped dill
	Salt and freshly ground pepper

1. To prepare the ravioli, prepare the pasta dough following the instructions on pages 16–25. Let rest, then roll out thinly. Cut into 4-inch (10-cm) disks.

2. To prepare the filling, combine the salmon, 1 tablespoon of egg white, cream, and dill in a food processor. Chop until smooth.

3. Sprinkle the cornstarch on a work surface and lay the disks of pasta out in rows of four. Brush every second disk around the edges with the remaining egg white.

4. Place a teaspoon of the salmon mixture in the middle of every other pasta disk. Lay the other disks on top. Press down around the mixture to seal.

5. Half-fill a large saucepan with water and the oil, bring to a boil, add the ravioli, and cook for 2–3 minutes.

6. To prepare the sauce, melt the butter in a large saucepan, add the flour, and cook for 1 minute. Add the wine, stir until smooth. Pour in the cream and lemon juice. Bring to a boil, then reduce until the sauce is a pouring consistency. Stir in the dill.

7. Put the ravioli in a hot serving dish and spoon the sauce over the top.

AMOUNT PER SERVING						
NUTRITION FACTS PERCENT DAILY VALUES (based on 2000 calories)	547 CALORIES 26%	22g PROTEIN 48%	11g FAT 14%	3g FIBER 12%	89g CARBS 68%	1.5g SALT 27%

ravioli with pumpkin sauce

To make pumpkin or winter squash purée, cut the pumpkin in half, stem to base. Remove the seeds and pulp. Cover each half with aluminum foil and bake in a hot oven, foil side up, until tender, about 45 minutes. Scrape the pumpkin flesh from the shell and purée in a blender.

 Serves 6

10 minutes

30 minutes

1

14	ounces (400 g) fresh or frozen ravioli with beef filling	
1	cup (250 ml) light (single) cream	
½	teaspoon ground nutmeg	
⅔	cup (150 g) canned pumpkin or winter squash or cooked	

pumpkin, puréed

2 tablespoons sour cream

¼ cup (30 g) grated Parmesan cheese

Handful of fresh chives, snipped

1. **Cook** the ravioli in a large pot of salted boiling water until al dente.

2. **To prepare the sauce,** heat the cream and nutmeg in a medium frying pan over a medium-high heat until reduced by half, about 5 minutes.

3. **Add** the pumpkin purée, sour cream, and Parmesan. Stir until combined, then reduce the heat to low. Add the ravioli, toss well, and serve hot garnished with the chives.

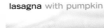

AMOUNT PER SERVING **NUTRITION FACTS** PERCENT DAILY VALUES (based on 2000 calories)	351 CALORIES 17%	13g PROTEIN 28%	14g FAT 17%	2g FIBER 8%	26g CARBS 20%	1.2g SALT 21%

If you liked this recipe, you will love these as well.

pappardelle with pumpkin & saffron

48

lasagna with pumpkin

110

tortellini with pancetta & leeks

Leeks are rich in vitamin A, C, and K and dietary fiber. They belong to the same family as garlic and onions and provide many of the same health benefits, such as improved heart function.

Serves 6

15 minutes

30 minutes

2

3	tablespoons (90 g) butter
2	large leeks, white parts thinly sliced, green leaves, chopped
1/3	cup (90 ml) dry vermouth
8	ounces (250 g) pancetta, diced
3/4	cup (180 ml) heavy (double) cream
1/2	cup (75 g) blanched pistachios, coarsely chopped

	Salt and freshly ground black pepper
14	ounces (400 g) fresh store-bought tortellini, with meat filling
4	tablespoons freshly grated Parmesan cheese
	Pinch of saffron strands
1	cup (125 g) smoked provolone or other firm smoked cheese, cut into small cubes

1. **Melt** the butter in a large frying pan over medium heat. Add the sliced leeks and sauté for 1 minute. Add the vermouth and let evaporate for 1 minute.

2. **Lower** the heat and simmer until the leeks are very tender, 10–12 minutes.

3. **Sauté** the pancetta in another frying pan over medium heat for 1 minute. Add the cream and simmer until the mixture has reduced slightly, 3–4 minutes.

4. **Add** the pistachios and cooked leeks. Mix well. Add the chopped leek leaves and mix again. Season with salt and pepper.

5. **Meanwhile**, cook the tortellini in a large saucepan of salted boiling water for 3–4 minutes, or until al dente. Drain and add to the pan with the sauce.

6. **Add** the Parmesan and saffron and toss gently over low heat. Add the provolone and toss again. Season with a little more pepper and serve hot.

AMOUNT PER SERVING	500	25g	32g	2g	22g	2.6g
NUTRITION FACTS	**CALORIES**	**PROTEIN**	**FAT**	**FIBER**	**CARBS**	**SALT**
PERCENT DAILY VALUES (based on 2000 calories)	25%	54%	40%	8%	17%	48%

If you liked this recipe, you will love these as well.

tortellini with woodcutters' sauce

98

spaghetti with pancetta, mozzarella & eggs

282

tortellini with woodcutters' sauce

This classic sauce is known in Italian as *alla boscaiolo* or woodcutters' sauce. There are many variations, but they always include mushrooms and cream.

 Serves 6

 15 minutes

 20 minutes

 2

14 ounces (400 g) fresh store-bought tortellini
2 tablespoons extra-virgin olive oil
8 ounces (250 g) button mushrooms, sliced
8 ounces (250 g) ham, coarsely chopped

1¼ cups (300 ml) light (single) cream
Finely grated zest of 1 lemon
2 tablespoons finely chopped fresh parsley
Salt and freshly ground black pepper

1. **Cook** the tortellini in a large pot of salted boiling water until al dente.

2. **To prepare the sauce,** heat the oil in a large frying pan over a medium heat. Sauté the mushrooms until soft, about 5 minutes.

3. **Add** the ham and simmer for 2 minutes.

4. **Drain** the tortellini and add to the pan with the mushrooms. Add the cream, lemon zest, and parsley. Season with salt and pepper.

5. **Stir** until heated through, about 2 minutes. Spoon into bowls and serve hot.

AMOUNT PER SERVING	373	18g	21g	3g	27g	1.7g
NUTRITION FACTS	**CALORIES**	**PROTEIN**	**FAT**	**FIBER**	**CARBS**	**SALT**
PERCENT DAILY VALUES (based on 2000 calories)	18%	39%	26%	12%	21%	31%

If you liked this recipe, you will love these as well.

fettuccine with cream & ham

36

tortellini with pancetta & leeks

96

baked rigatoni with ham & mushrooms

218

tortellini with fava beans

Fava beans (also known as broad beans) come into season in the early spring. They are packed with riboflavin, niacin, phosphorus, potassium, folate, copper, and manganese.

- Serves 6
- 15 minutes
- 20 minutes

 2

1½	pounds (750 g) fresh cheese tortellini
2	pounds (1 kg) fresh fava (broad) beans in pod
	Salt and freshly ground black pepper
⅓	cup (90 ml) extra-virgin olive oil
1	cup (50 g) arugula (rocket) leaves
⅔	cup (150 g) feta cheese, crumbled

1. Cook the tortellini in a large pot of salted boiling water until al dente. Drain and return to the pan.

2. Meanwhile, cook the fava beans in a saucepan of boiling water until just tender, 3–5 minutes. Drain and rinse in cold water.

3. Remove and discard the tough outer skins. Add the fava beans to the hot tortellini. Season with salt and pepper.

4. Add the oil, arugula, and feta. Toss over low heat until well combined. Serve hot.

AMOUNT PER SERVING	626	26g	33g	12g	58g	1g
NUTRITION FACTS	CALORIES	PROTEIN	FAT	FIBER	CARBS	SALT
PERCENT DAILY VALUES (based on 2000 calories)	30%	57%	41%	48%	45%	17%

If you liked this recipe, you will love these as well.

ravioli with olive pesto

90

whole-wheat spaghetti with zucchini & bell peppers

258

baked pasta with eggs

These pretty little pasta dishes make an enticing entrée. Use whole-wheat or spinach fettuccine, if preferred.

Serves 6

20 minutes

Time for pasta

1 hour

2

14	ounces (400 g) homemade or store-bought fettuccine

SAUCE

3	tablespoons butter
3	tablespoons all-purpose (plain) flour
2	cups (500 ml) beef stock
2	tablespoons freshly grated Parmesan
2	tablespoons coarsely grated Emmental (Swiss) cheese
1/3	cup (60 ml) heavy (double) cream
	Salt and freshly ground white pepper
1	pinch freshly ground nutmeg

TOPPING

3	tablespoons butter
1/2	cup (50 g) chopped zucchini (courgettes)
1/2	cup (50 g) cubed carrots
1/2	cup (50 g) asparagus spears, cut into short lengths
1/2	cup (50 g) cubed white mushrooms
3	tablespoons water
	Salt and freshly ground white pepper
6	small eggs
4	tablespoons freshly grated Parmesan cheese

1. **If using homemade pasta,** prepare the fettuccine following the instructions on pages 16–25.

2. **To prepare the sauce,** melt the butter in a large saucepan. Add the flour and stir to form a smooth paste. Cook, stirring, for 1 minute.

3. **Pour in** the stock, whisking to prevent lumps from forming. Bring to a boil and simmer over low heat, stirring almost constantly, until thickened, about 10 minutes. Let cool. Stir in the Parmesan, Emmental, and cream. Season with salt, white pepper, and nutmeg.

4. **To prepare the topping,** melt the butter in a large frying pan. Add the vegetables and water and simmer until the vegetables are tender. Season with

salt and white pepper and remove from the heat.

5. **Cook** the pasta in a large pot of salted boiling water for half the time indicated on the package. Drain well. Toss with the vegetables and the cheese sauce.

6. **Preheat** the oven to 400°F (200°C/ gas 6). Butter six individual baking dishes.

7. **Use** a large fork to make six nests of fettuccine and place them in the dishes. Break an egg into the center of each one. Season with salt and white pepper.

8. **Sprinkle** with the Parmesan and bake for 15–20 minutes, or until the eggs are cooked. Serve piping hot.

AMOUNT PER SERVING	420	15g	19g	2g	51g	0.7g
NUTRITION FACTS	CALORIES	PROTEIN	FAT	FIBER	CARBS	SALT
PERCENT DAILY VALUES (based on 2000 calories)	20%	33%	23%	8%	39%	12%

pizzocheri with cabbage

Pizzoccheri come from the Valtellina, an Alpine valley in northern Italy. Made from a mixture of buckwheat and ordinary flour, they are richer in fiber than normal fresh pasta.

Serves 6

1 hour

30 minutes

45 minutes

3

PASTA DOUGH

2⅓ cups (350 g) buckwheat flour

2 cups (300 g) all-purpose (plain) flour

3 large eggs

½ cup (125 ml) milk

1 teaspoon salt

FILLING

8 ounces (250 g) potatoes, cut into small cubes

6 ounces (180 g) Savoy or green cabbage, shredded

⅓ cup (90 g) butter

2 cloves garlic, finely chopped

4 leaves fresh sage
Freshly ground black pepper

¾ cup (75 g) freshly grated Parmesan cheese

½ cup (120 g) thinly sliced Fontina cheese

1. **To prepare the pasta,** combine both flours in a large bowl. Add the eggs, milk, and salt and stir to obtain a firm dough.

2. **Transfer** the dough to a lightly floured work surface and knead until smooth, about 10 minutes. Set aside for 30 minutes.

3. **Roll** the pasta out until about ⅛ inch (3 mm) thick. Roll the sheet of pasta loosely and cut into strips ¼ inch (5 mm) wide and 3 inches (8 cm) long.

4. **Preheat** the oven to 350°F (180°C/gas 4). Bring a large pot of lightly salted water to a boil. Add the potatoes and cook for 5 minutes, then add the cabbage. When the potatoes are almost ready, add the

pasta. When the vegetables and pasta are cooked, drain carefully.

5. **Melt** the butter with the garlic and sage in a small saucepan over medium-low heat. Cook for 2 minutes.

6. **Butter** a large ovenproof dish. Place the pasta and vegetables in the dish. Drizzle with a little butter, sprinkle with pepper and Parmesan and cover with Fontina.

7. **Repeat** this layering process two or three times until all the ingredients are in the dish. Finish with a layer of Parmesan.

8. **Bake** until the cheese is golden brown on top, about 25 minutes. Serve hot.

AMOUNT PER SERVING	748 CALORIES	24g PROTEIN	28g FAT	5g FIBER	106g CARBS	1.7g SALT
NUTRITION FACTS PERCENT DAILY VALUES (based on 2000 calories)	36%	52%	35%	20%	82%	31%

lasagna stacks with pesto

Try to buy organic vine-ripened tomatoes to ensure top quality in taste and freshness. Don't chop the pesto too finely; it should be pleasantly nutty.

Serve 6

40 minutes

Time for pasta

10 minutes

2

LASAGNA

14	ounces (400 g) fresh lasagna sheets
2	ounces (60 g) baby spinach leaves
4	large vine-ripened tomatoes, cut into thick slices
4	large bocconcini (mozzarella), cut into thick slices
8	fresh basil leaves

PESTO

2	cloves garlic
2	tablespoons pine nuts, toasted
1	bunch fresh basil leaves
2	tablespoons finely grated Parmesan cheese
½	cup (125 ml) extra-virgin olive oil

1. **If using homemade pasta,** prepare the lasagna sheets following the instructions on pages 16–25.

2. **To prepare the pesto,** combine the garlic, pine nuts, basil, and Parmesan in a food processor and process until coarsely chopped.

3. **With the motor running,** gradually add the oil and process until the mixture is smooth and well mixed.

4. **Cut** the lasagna sheets into 12 x 3-inch (30 x 7-cm) rectangles. Cook in a large pot of salted boiling water until al dente, 3–4 minutes. Drain well.

5. **Place** one sheet in the center of each serving plate and top with a couple of spinach leaves, a slice each of tomato and bocconcini, a fresh basil leaf, and a spoonful of pesto.

6. **Top** with another sheet of lasagna and layer as before, finishing with a layer of lasagna. Each stack should have two complete layers. Place a generous spoonful of pesto on top of each stack and serve immediately.

AMOUNT PER SERVING	661	30g	38g	3g	53g	1.1g
NUTRITION FACTS	CALORIES	PROTEIN	FAT	FIBER	CARBS	SALT
PERCENT DAILY VALUES (based on 2 000 calories)	32%	65%	47%	12%	41%	20%

If you liked this recipe, you will love these as well.

farfalle with cherry tomatoes & olives

114

pasta salad with baby mozzarella & tomatoes

124

spaghetti with pancetta, mozzarella & eggs

282

lasagna with meatballs

This is a very special lasagna—originally from southern Italy where it was served on feast days. It is very filling and can be served as a meal in itself.

 Serves 8

 1 hour

 Time for pasta

 2 hours 30 minutes

 3

14	ounces (400 g) homemade or store-bought lasagna
	Meat Sauce (see page 208)

MEATBALLS

12	ounces (350 g) ground (minced) beef
2	large eggs
2	tablespoons freshly grated pecorino cheese
	Salt and freshly ground
	black pepper
1	cup (250 g) mozzarella cheese, sliced
3	hard-boiled eggs, finely chopped
¾	cup (90 g) freshly grated pecorino cheese
2	tablespoons chilled butter, cut into flakes

1. **If using homemade pasta**, prepare the lasagna sheets following the instructions on pages 16–25.

2. **Blanch** the lasagna sheets in simmering water for 1 minute and lay out on a damp cloth.

3. **Prepare** the meat sauce. Preheat the oven to 400°F (200°C/gas 6). Oil an ovenproof baking dish.

4. **To prepare the meatballs,** mix the beef, eggs, and pecorino in a large bowl. Season with salt and pepper and form into balls the size of hazelnuts.

5. **Add** the meatballs to the meat sauce and cook for 10 minutes.

6. **Lay** the first layer of lasagna in the prepared baking dish. Cover with some of the meat sauce, mozzarella, eggs, and pecorino. Continue to layer the ingredients for a total of five layers, finishing with a layer of pasta.

7. **Dot** with the butter and sprinkle with any remaining pecorino. Bake for 35–40 minutes, or until golden brown. Let rest at room temperature for 15 minutes before serving.

AMOUNT PER SERVING	955	39g	71g	3g	41g	1.2g
NUTRITION FACTS	**CALORIES**	**PROTEIN**	**FAT**	**FIBER**	**CARBS**	**SALT**
PERCENT DAILY VALUES (based on 2 000 calories)	46%	85%	88%	12%	32%	23%

If you liked this recipe, you will love these as well.

fettuccine with meatballs

70

lasagna with pumpkin

110

spaghetti with meatballs

306

lasagna with winter squash

This delicious vegetarian lasagna has layers of pumpkin, rosemary, and garlic, a creamy Béchamel sauce, and a rich cream and Parmesan topping.

Serves 8

1 hour

Time for pasta

70 minutes

3

14	ounces (400 g) fresh lasagna sheets
1	small butternut winter squash (pumpkin)
2	large sprigs fresh rosemary
3	cloves garlic, finely chopped
2	tablespoons extra-virgin olive oil + extra, to grease
	Salt and pepper
1/4	cup (60 g) butter
4	tablespoons all-purpose (plain) flour
4	cups (1 liter) milk
1	cup (125 g) freshly grated Parmesan cheese + 1/2 cup (60 g) for the topping
1/2	cup (125 ml) heavy (double) cream

1. If using homemade pasta, prepare the lasagna sheets following the instructions on pages 16–25.

2. Preheat the oven to 425°F (220°C/gas 7). Peel the winter squash, remove the seeds, and cut into small cubes.

3. Combine the winter squash in a large bowl with the rosemary, garlic, oil, salt, and pepper, and toss thoroughly. Transfer to an ovenproof baking dish and bake for 25 minutes or until golden brown.

4. Meanwhile, melt the butter in a saucepan, add the flour, and stir until the flour absorbs the butter. When golden brown, add the milk and whisk while reheating (It may appear to have lumps initially, but these will disappear as the liquid heats.) Keep stirring and simmering until thick. Add the winter squash mixture and mix thoroughly.

5. Lightly oil a lasagna (or baking) dish and ladle just enough sauce over the base of the dish to cover it. Place a layer of lasagna sheets over the sauce and cover with another layer of sauce.

6. Sprinkle with cheese, then cover with another layer of lasagna sheets. Continue layering until all the sauce, lasagna, and cheese has been used, ending with lasagna sheets.

7. Whip the cream, add a little salt, then spread the salted cream over the top lasagna sheet. Sprinkle with the extra Parmesan cheese, then cover with foil.

8. Put the lasagna in the oven, then reduce the heat to 350°F (180°C/gas 4) and bake for 30 minutes.

9. Remove the foil and continue baking for 15 minutes. Remove the lasagna from the oven and let rest for 5 minutes. Serve warm.

AMOUNT PER SERVING					
NUTRITION FACTS	477 CALORIES	17g PROTEIN	28g FAT	1g FIBER	43g CARBS	0.6g SALT
PERCENT DAILY VALUES (based on 2000 calories)	23%	37%	35%	4%	33%	10%

Short
Pasta

farfalle salad with cherry tomatoes & olives

Anchovies, both whole and fillets, are readily available in 2-ounce (60-g) cans in most supermarkets. Salted anchovies can be found in Italian delicatessens and markets.

Serves 6

15 minutes

30 minutes

15–20 minutes

1

1	pound (500 g) farfalle	1	cup (50 g) black olives, pitted
¼	cup (60 ml) extra-virgin olive oil	2	tablespoons finely chopped fresh basil
20	cherry tomatoes, halved	2	cloves garlic, finely chopped
1	tablespoon capers preserved in salt, rinsed	4	anchovy fillets preserved in oil, drained
8	ounces (250 g) fresh mozzarella, drained and cut into small cubes		

1. **Cook** the pasta in a large pot of salted boiling water until al dente. Drain and cool under cold running water. Drain the pasta again and dry on a clean kitchen towel.

2. **Transfer** to a large salad bowl. Add 2 tablespoons of the oil and toss well. Add the tomatoes, capers, mozzarella, olives, and basil. Mix well.

3. **Heat** the remaining oil in a small frying pan over medium heat. Add the garlic

and sauté until pale golden brown, 3–4 minutes.

4. **Add** the anchovies and sauté, crushing with a fork, until dissolved in the oil, 2–3 minutes.

5. **Drizzle** this mixture over the pasta salad and toss well. Chill for 30 minutes before serving.

AMOUNT PER SERVING	445	17g	20g	3g	54g	0.9g
NUTRITION FACTS	**CALORIES**	**PROTEIN**	**FAT**	**FIBER**	**CARBS**	**SALT**
PERCENT DAILY VALUES (based on 2 000 calories)	21%	37%	25%	12%	42%	16%

If you liked this recipe, you will love these as well.

pappardelle caprese

28

penne with cherry tomatoes

14

pasta salad with baby mozzarella & tomatoes

124

fusilli salad with bell peppers & arugula

Bell peppers (capsicums) are packed with nutrients, including vitamins C, K, and B6, beta-carotene, thiamine, folic acid, and many phytochemicals with strong antioxidant properties.

 Serves 6

 20 minutes

 40 minutes

 1

1 pound (500 g) fusilli or rotini
½ cup (125 ml) extra-virgin olive oil
2 red bell peppers (capsicum), seeded and cut 4–6 pieces lengthwise
1 yellow bell pepper (capsicum), seeded and cut 4–6 pieces lengthwise
1 bunch arugula (rocket), chopped

¾ cup (90 g) freshly grated aged pecorino or Parmesan cheese
10 basil leaves, torn
2 tablespoons freshly squeezed lemon juice
Salt and freshly ground black pepper

1. **Cook** the pasta in a large pot of salted boiling water until al dente. Drain and cool under cold running water. Drain the pasta again and dry on a clean kitchen towel. Put in a serving bowl with 2 tablespoons of oil. Toss gently.

2. **Cook** the bell peppers under a hot broiler (grill), turning often, until the skins are blackened.

3. **Place** in a plastic bag, shut tight, and leave for 10 minutes. Open the bag and peel away the skins. Clean off any blackened skins with paper towels. Don't rinse the bell peppers as this will remove much of their delicious flavor.

4. **Cut** the bell peppers into thin strips. Add to the pasta bowl together with the arugula, cheese, and basil. Toss gently.

5. **Pour** the remaining oil into a small bowl with the lemon juice, salt, and pepper and beat together. Drizzle over the salad. Toss well and serve.

AMOUNT PER SERVING **NUTRITION FACTS** PERCENT DAILY VALUES (based on 2 000 calories)	545 CALORIES 26%	17g PROTEIN 37%	25g FAT 31%	4g FIBER 16%	67g CARBS 52%	0.3g SALT 5%

If you liked this recipe, you will love these as well.

pasta salad with eggplant & pine nuts
122

fusilli with spinach & bell peppers
148

spaghetti with bell peppers & pancetta
260

grapefruit pasta salad

The ditalini pasta in this recipe is a type of maccheroni, more frequently used in soups such as minestrone. Pink grapefruits have a fresh, but not acidic flavor and add color to the dish.

 Serves 4

 25 minutes

 1 hour

 15 minutes

 1

2	large pink grapefruit
2	cups (400 g) canned corn (sweetcorn), drained
2	tablespoons extra-virgin olive oil
2	tablespoons mayonnaise
	Salt and freshly ground white pepper
12	ounces (350 g) ditalini or other short tube pasta
1	bunch fresh basil, torn
	Fresh mint leaves to garnish

1. **Cut** the grapefruit in half and remove the flesh. Chop coarsely. Wrap the empty skins in plastic wrap (cling film) and refrigerate until ready to use.

2. **Mix** the corn, grapefruit flesh, oil, and mayonnaise in a large bowl. Season with salt and white pepper.

3. **Cook** the pasta in a large pot of salted boiling water until al dente. Drain and run under cold running water. Drain again and dry on a clean kitchen towel.

4. **Put** the pasta in the bowl with the grapefruit mixture and toss gently. Add the basil. Refrigerate for 1 hour.

5. **Remove** the grapefruit skins from the refrigerator and fill with the pasta mixture. Garnish with the mint leaves and serve.

AMOUNT PER SERVING	CALORIES	PROTEIN	FAT	FIBER	CARBS	SALT
NUTRITION FACTS	402	11g	12g	3g	67g	0.1g
PERCENT DAILY VALUES (based on 2 000 calories)	19%	24%	15%	12%	52%	1%

If you liked this recipe, you will love these ones too:

penne with ricotta, zucchini & orange

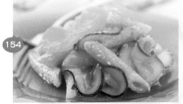
154

spaghetti with tomato & lemon

254

cool fusilli with tomatoes & onion

For extra flavor, add diced cheese or flakes of Parmesan to this simple pasta salad.

Serves 6

15 minutes

30 minutes

15 minutes

1

1	pound (500 g) fusilli or rotini
1/3	cup (90 ml) extra-virgin olive oil
1 1/2	pounds (750 g) firm ripe beefsteak (salad) tomatoes, peeled and coarsely chopped
1	large sweet red Spanish onion, finely chopped
2	cloves garlic, finely chopped
3	tablespoons finely chopped fresh basil
1–2	dried chiles, crumbled (optional)
	Salt

1. **Cook** the pasta in a large pot of salted boiling water until al dente. Drain and run under cold running water. Drain again and dry on a clean kitchen towel. Transfer to a large salad bowl.

2. **Add** 2 tablespoons of oil and toss well. Add the tomatoes, onion, garlic, basil, chiles, if using, and the remaining oil.

3. **Season** with salt and toss well. Serve at room temperature or chill in the refrigerator for 30 minutes.

AMOUNT PER SERVING	437 CALORIES	11g PROTEIN	15g FAT	6g FIBER	68g CARBS	0.1g SALT
NUTRITION FACTS PERCENT DAILY VALUES (based on 2000 calories)	21%	24%	19%	24%	52%	1%

If you liked this recipe, you will love these as well.

farfalle with cherry tomatoes & olives
114

maccheroni with onion sauce
138

pasta salad with eggplant & pine nuts
122

pasta salad with eggplant & pine nuts

Eggplant belongs to the same family as tomatoes and potatoes. It is an excellent source of dietary fiber and a good source of vitamins B1, B6, and potassium.

Serves 6

30 minutes

1 hour

20 minutes

2

1	large eggplant (aubergine), with skin, cut into ½-inch (1-cm) thick slices
	Coarse sea salt
2	cups (500 ml) olive oil, for frying
2	yellow bell peppers (capsicums)
⅓	cup (90 ml) extra-virgin olive oil
1	large onion, finely chopped
2	cloves garlic, finely chopped
	Salt

2	tablespoons pine nuts
1	pound (500 g) ditalini or other short tube pasta
2	tablespoons salt-cured capers, rinsed
1	cup (100 g) green olives, pitted and coarsely chopped
1	small bunch fresh basil, torn
2	tablespoons finely chopped fresh parsley
1	tablespoon finely chopped fresh oregano

1. Put the eggplant in a colander and sprinkle with the coarse sea salt. Allow to drain for 1 hour, then chop into small cubes.

2. Heat the oil in a large frying pan over medium-high heat. Fry the eggplant in batches until tender and golden brown, 5–7 minutes each batch. Drain on paper towels.

3. Cook the bell peppers under a hot broiler (grill), turning often, until the skins are blackened.

4. Put in a plastic bag, shut tight, and leave for 10 minutes. Open the bag and peel away the skins. Clean off any blackened skins with paper towels. Don't rinse the bell peppers as this will remove much of their delicious flavor. Cut into small squares.

4. Heat 3 tablespoons of the extra-virgin oil in a small saucepan over medium heat. Add the onion and garlic with a pinch of salt and sauté until golden brown, about 5 minutes. Cover and simmer over low heat for 15 minutes.

5. Toast the pine nuts in a nonstick frying pan over medium heat until golden, 3–4 minutes.

6. Meanwhile, cook the pasta in a large pot of salted boiling water until al dente. Drain and let cool under running cold water. Drain again and dry on a clean kitchen towel.

7. Transfer to a large serving bowl and toss well with the fried eggplant, capers, bell peppers, onions, pine nuts, olives, basil, parsley, and oregano. Serve hot.

AMOUNT PER SERVING					
NUTRITION FACTS					
PERCENT DAILY VALUES (based on 2 000 calories)					

 547 CALORIES 26% 12g PROTEIN 26% 27g FAT 33% 3g FIBER 12% 69g CARBS 53% 0.9g SALT 17%

penne with bell peppers, eggplant & zucchini

The pasta in this dish provides the perfect counterpoint to the intense flavors of the freshly grilled vegetables, herbs, and oil. Try it with whole-wheat (wholemeal) penne, too.

- Serves 6
- 45 minutes
- 2 hours
- 30 minutes

- 2

1	pound (500 g) penne
1/3	cup (90 ml) extra-virgin olive oil
1	large red bell peppers (capsicum), seeded, cored, and quartered
1	large eggplant (aubergine), with skin, thinly sliced
2	zucchini (courgettes) thinly sliced lengthwise
12	leaves fresh basil, torn
1	tablespoon finely chopped fresh mint
1	clove garlic, finely chopped
1/2	teaspoon finely grated fresh ginger
	Salt and freshly ground black pepper

1. **Cook** the pasta in a large pot of salted boiling water until al dente. Drain and run under cold running water. Drain again and dry in a clean kitchen towel. Transfer to a large salad bowl and toss with 2 tablespoons of oil.

2. **Turn on** the broiler (grill) and broil the bell peppers, turning them often, until the skins are blackened. Wrap in a brown paper bag or foil for 10 minutes. Take out of the bag or foil and peel off the skins.

3. **Heat** a grill pan. Cook the eggplant and zucchini in batches until tender, 5–8 minutes each batch.

4. **Chop** all the vegetables coarsely. Add to the salad bowl with the pasta and toss gently.

5. **Add** the basil, mint, garlic, and ginger. Season with salt and pepper and drizzle with the remaining oil. Mix and let stand for 2 hours before serving.

AMOUNT PER SERVING	430	12g	15g	4g	65g	0.1g
NUTRITION FACTS	**CALORIES**	**PROTEIN**	**FAT**	**FIBER**	**CARBS**	**SALT**
PERCENT DAILY VALUES (based on 2 000 calories)	21%	26%	19%	16%	50%	2%

If you liked this recipe, you will love these as well.

fusilli with spinach and bell peppers
148

whole-wheat spaghetti with summer vegetables
266

spaghetti with zucchini
246

pasta salad with tuna & olives

This healthy dish is ideal for summer meals. It can be prepared ahead of time and chilled in the refrigerator until ready to serve. Use whole-wheat (wholemeal) pasta, if preferred.

 Serves 6

30 minutes

1 hour

15 minutes

1

20	cherry tomatoes, halved
	Salt
5	ounces (150 g) canned tuna, packed in oil, drained
12	black olives
6	green olives, pitted and chopped
2	scallions (spring onions), coarsely chopped
1	stalk celery, sliced
1	carrot, coarsely chopped

1	clove garlic, finely chopped
1/3	cup (90 ml) extra-virgin olive oil
	Freshly ground white pepper
1	pound (500 g) penne
2	teaspoons dried oregano
1	tablespoon finely chopped fresh parsley
	Fresh basil, torn

1. **Sprinkle** the tomatoes with salt. Put in a colander and let drain for 1 hour.

2. **Put** the tuna in a large salad bowl and crumble with a fork. Add the tomatoes, olives, scallions, celery, carrot, and garlic. Drizzle with almost all of the oil and season with salt, white pepper, and oregano.

3. **Meanwhile,** cook the pasta in a large pot of salted boiling water until al dente. Drain and cool under cold running water. Drain the pasta again and dry on a clean kitchen towel.

4. **Transfer** to the bowl with the tomatoes and other ingredients and drizzle with the remaining oil. Add the parsley and basil and toss well. Serve at room temperature.

AMOUNT PER SERVING	423	16g	16g	3g	57g	0.6g
NUTRITION FACTS	**CALORIES**	**PROTEIN**	**FAT**	**FIBER**	**CARBS**	**SALT**
PERCENT DAILY VALUES (based on 2 000 calories)	20%	35%	20%	12%	44%	11%

If you liked this recipe, you will love these as well.

pasta salad with fresh tuna

130

pasta with tuna sauce

182

pasta salad with fresh tuna

Tuna is an excellent source of protein, vitamin B12, potassium, and selenium. Bluefin tuna is also very rich in omega-3 fatty acids.

Serves 6

20 minutes

30 minutes

12–15 minutes

1

14	ounces (400 g) fresh tuna, in a single slice, skinned, boned, and chopped in ¾-inch (1.5-cm) cubes
	Freshly squeezed juice of 1 lemon
½	cup (125 ml) extra-virgin olive oil
20	black olives, pitted and chopped

2	cloves garlic, lightly crushed but whole
1	pound (500 g) tomatoes, peeled and chopped
	Salt and freshly ground white pepper
1	pound (500 g) conchiglie or medium shells
	Fresh basil leaves, torn

1. **Put** the tuna in a bowl. Drizzle with the lemon juice and ¼ cup (60 ml) of the oil. Add the olives. Let marinate for 30 minutes.

2. **Heat** ¼ cup (60 ml) of oil in a large frying pan over medium heat. Add the garlic and sauté for 1–2 minutes. Remove from the heat and let cool. Discard the garlic.

3. **Coarsely chop** the tomatoes, sprinkle with salt, and put in a colander. Let drain for 15 minutes.

4. **Mix** the tomatoes and garlic-infused oil into the bowl with the tuna. Season with salt and white pepper.

5. **Cook** the pasta in a large pot of salted boiling water until al dente. Drain and let cool under running cold water. Drain again and dry on a clean kitchen towel.

6. **Transfer** to a serving bowl. Add the tuna sauce and basil. Toss well and serve.

AMOUNT PER SERVING	561	26g	24g	4g	64g	0.6g
NUTRITION FACTS	CALORIES	PROTEIN	FAT	FIBER	CARBS	SALT
PERCENT DAILY VALUES (based on 2 000 calories)	27%	57%	30%	16%	49%	11%

If you liked this recipe, you will love these as well.

pasta salad with tuna & olives

128

spaghetti with tuna & capers

286

farfalline with grilled vegetables

Farfalline are a smaller version of bow-tie or farfalle (butterfly-shaped) pasta. If preferred, replace with standard farfalle or penne. Baby corn cobs add crunch and texture to this dish.

Serves 6

15 minutes

30 minutes

1

2	zucchini (courgettes), thinly sliced lengthwise
1	eggplant (aubergine), with skin, thinly sliced
4	large red salad tomatoes
12	ears baby corn (sweet corn)
1	pound (500 g) farfalline or tripolini

8	ounces (250 g) fresh mozzarella cheese, cut into small cubes
1–2	tablespoons finely chopped fresh mint
	Salt and freshly ground black pepper
¼	cup (60 ml) extra-virgin olive oil

1. **Heat** a grill pan over high heat. Grill the zucchini and eggplant slices in batches until tender, 5–8 minutes per batch.

2. **Blanch** the tomatoes in boiling water for 1 minute. Slip off the skins. Chop coarsely. Blanch the baby corn cobs in salted, boiling water for 1 minute. Drain and set aside.

3. **Cook** the pasta in a large pot of salted boiling water until al dente. Drain well and toss with the vegetables, mozzarella, and mint. Season with salt and pepper and drizzle with the oil.

4. **Serve** hot or at room temperature.

AMOUNT PER SERVING NUTRITION FACTS PERCENT DAILY VALUES (based on 2 000 calories)	496 CALORIES 24%	19g PROTEIN 41%	19g FAT 23%	4g FIBER 16%	65g CARBS 50%	0.4g SALT 7%

If you liked this recipe, you will love these as well.

pasta with raw zucchini, pecorino & mint

134

penne with bell peppers, eggplant & zucchini

126

whole-wheat spaghetti with summer vegetables

256

penne with raw zucchini, pecorino & mint

The smaller and younger the zucchini, the more tender and sweet they will be. This dish is best served in spring and summer when zucchini are in season and at their best.

 Serves 6

20 minutes

20–30 minutes

10–12 minutes

 1

6	very fresh small zucchini (courgettes)
2	tablespoons freshly squeezed lemon juice
	Salt and freshly ground black pepper
1/3	cup (90 ml) extra-virgin olive oil

Small bunch fresh mint leaves

| 1 | pound (500 g) penne |
| 1 | cup (125 g) freshly grated aged pecorino or Parmesan cheese, cubed |

1. **Cut** the zucchini lengthwise in julienne strips and put in a large bowl.

2. **Add** the lemon juice, salt, pepper, oil, and mint leaves. Stir well and let sit for 20–30 minutes.

3. **Cook** the pasta in a large pot of salted boiling water until al dente.

4. **Drain well** and place in the bowl with the zucchini. Toss well and serve with the cheese passed separately.

AMOUNT PER SERVING	505	19g	21g	3g	63g	0.4g
NUTRITION FACTS	CALORIES	PROTEIN	FAT	FIBER	CARBS	SALT
PERCENT DAILY VALUES (based on 2 000 calories)	25%	41%	26%	12%	48%	7%

If you liked this recipe, you will love these as well.

farfalline with grilled vegetables

132

whole-wheat spaghetti with summer vegetables

256

spaghetti with zucchini

246

maccheroni with chocolate nut sauce

This unusual dish comes from northeastern Italy where several different pasta dishes are made with cocoa or chocolate.

Serves 6

10 minutes

10–15 minutes

1

1 pound (500 g) maccheroni (macarconi) or other short pasta shape
1/3 cup (90 g) butter
1/3 cup (70 g) sugar
2½ cups (300 g) finely chopped walnuts
½ cup (75 g) unsweetened cocoa powder

1 cup (125 g) fine dry bread crumbs
½ teaspoon ground cinnamon
Finely grated zest of 1 large lemon

1. **Cook** the pasta in a large pot of salted boiling water until al dente. Drain and transfer to a large bowl.

2. **Stir in** the butter. Add the sugar, walnuts, cocoa, bread crumbs, cinnamon, and lemon zest and toss well. Serve hot.

AMOUNT PER SERVING NUTRITION FACTS PERCENT DAILY VALUES (based on 2 000 calories)	813 CALORIES 39%	20g PROTEIN 43%	48g FAT 59%	5g FIBER 20%	81g CARBS 62%	0.7g SALT 12%

If you liked this recipe, you will love these as well.

Whole-wheat penne with tuna, avocado & fresh herbs

180

maccheroni with onion sauce

Onions, like garlic and leeks, are part of the lily family. Eating them brings many and varied health benefits, including the prevention of blood clots and the lowering of artery-clogging cholesterol. Other studies suggest that onions may help lower blood pressure and prevent cancer.

Serves 6

10 minutes

55 minutes

2

- ¼ cup (60 ml) extra-virgin olive oil
- ¼ cup (60 g) butter
- 5 large white onions, thinly sliced
  Salt and freshly ground black pepper
- 1 cup (250 ml) dry white wine

- 1 pound (500 g) maccheroni (macaroni)
- 2 tablespoons finely chopped fresh parsley
- 6 tablespoons freshly grated Parmesan cheese

1. **Heat** the oil in a small frying pan over medium heat. Add the butter and sauté the onions until they begin to change color, 5–7 minutes. Season with salt and pepper.

2. **Turn** the heat down to low, cover, and simmer until the onions are soft and caramelized, about 40 minutes.

3. **Add** the wine. Turn the heat up to medium and stir until the wine evaporates. Remove from the heat.

4. **Meanwhile,** cook the pasta in a large pot of salted boiling water until al dente. Drain well and transfer to a heated serving dish.

5. **Pour** the onion sauce over the top. Add the parsley and Parmesan and toss well. Serve hot.

AMOUNT PER SERVING	570	16g	22g	5g	75g	0.3g
NUTRITION FACTS	CALORIES	PROTEIN	FAT	FIBER	CARBS	SALT
PERCENT DAILY VALUES (based on 2000 calories)	27%	35%	27%	20%	58%	6%

If you liked this recipe, you will love these as well.

cool fusilli with tomatoes & onion

120

spaghettini with fresh herbs

248

penne with cherry tomatoes

Recent research has shown that the lycopene found in tomatoes is extremely effective in protecting against many types of cancer. Cooking does not destroy lycopene and may even enhance its concentration.

Serves 6

15 minutes

30 minutes

1

⅓	cup (90 ml) extra-virgin olive oil
3	cloves garlic, whole but lightly crushed
1	pound (500 g) cherry tomatoes, halved
	Salt and freshly ground black pepper

⅓	cup (60 g) pine nuts
1	pound (500 g) plain or whole-wheat (wholemeal) penne
8	ounces (250 g) fresh baby spinach

1. Heat the oil in a large frying pan over medium heat. Add the garlic and sauté until pale golden brown, 3–4 minutes. Remove the garlic and discard.

2. Add the cherry tomatoes and sauté over high heat for 5 minutes. Season with salt and pepper. Remove from the heat and set aside.

3. Toast the pine nuts in a small frying pan over a medium-high heat. Do not add any oil or fat to the pan.

4. Meanwhile, cook the penne in a large pot of salted boiling water for 7–8 minutes. Add the spinach and continue cooking until the pasta is al dente.

5. Drain the penne and spinach and add to the frying pan with the cherry tomatoes. Toss over high heat for 2–3 minutes.

6. Add the pine nuts, season with a generous grinding of pepper, and serve hot.

AMOUNT PER SERVING	486	15g	23g	9g	59g	0.4g
NUTRITION FACTS	CALORIES	PROTEIN	FAT	FIBER	CARBS	SALT
PERCENT DAILY VALUES (based on 2000 calories)	23%	33%	28%	36%	45%	7%

If you liked this recipe, you will love these as well.

fettuccine with roasted tomato sauce

40

penne with bell peppers, eggplant & zucchini

126

farfalle with yogurt sauce & avocado

Chiles (also known as chilis, chillis, and chilli peppers) are believed to contain phytochemicals that help ward off cancer, lower cholesterol, and reduce weight.

 Serves 6

30 minutes

20 minutes

1

1	pound (500 g) farfalle
1	tablespoon dry white wine
¼	cup (60 ml) extra-virgin olive oil
2	cloves garlic, finely chopped
1	large onion, chopped
1	ripe avocado, peeled, pitted, and chopped
	Freshly squeezed juice of 1 lime

1	cup (250 ml) plain yogurt
	Salt and freshly ground black pepper
1	fresh red chile, thinly sliced
1	heart celery, thinly sliced
2	tablespoons salt-cured capers, rinsed
1	tablespoon finely chopped fresh parsley

1. Cook the pasta in a large pot of salted boiling water until al dente.

2. While the pasta is cooking, heat 2 tablespoons of oil in a frying pan over medium heat. Add the garlic and onion and sauté until pale gold, 3–4 minutes. Add the wine and simmer until evaporated. Set aside.

3. Drizzle the avocado with the lemon juice to prevent it from browning.

4. Beat the yogurt with the remaining oil in a large bowl. Season with salt and pepper. Add the chile, celery, capers, and parsley.

5. Drain the pasta well and transfer to a large serving bowl. Add the yogurt and onion mixtures and avocado and toss well. Serve hot.

AMOUNT PER SERVING	442	13g	15g	4g	57g	0.1g
NUTRITION FACTS	CALORIES	PROTEIN	FAT	FIBER	CARBS	SALT
PERCENT DAILY VALUES (based on 2 000 calories)	21%	28%	19%	16%	44%	2%

If you liked this recipe, you will love these as well.

whole-wheat penne with avocado & fresh herbs

180

spaghetti with yogurt & avocado

238

pasta with tomatoes, ricotta & pesto

Ricotta is a whey cheese, made from the liquid that separates out from the curds during the cheesemaking process. Ricotta is naturally low in fat and salt.

Serves 6

15 minutes

40 minutes

1

1	pound (500 g) rigatoni	
¼	cup (60 ml) extra-virgin olive oil	
4	cloves garlic, finely chopped	
1	pound (500 g) cherry tomatoes, halved	
12	ounces (350 g) very fresh ricotta cheese, drained	

Pesto (see page 106)
Salt and freshly ground black pepper
Fresh basil leaves, to garnish

1. **Cook** the pasta in a large pot of salted boiling water until al dente.

2. **While the pasta is cooking,** heat the oil in a large frying pan over medium heat. Add the garlic and sauté until pale gold, 2–3 minutes.

3. **Add** the cherry tomatoes and simmer over low heat until just softened, 3–5 minutes.

4. **Drain** the pasta and place in a heated serving dish. Add the ricotta, pesto, and tomatoes. Season with salt and pepper. Toss gently, garnish with the basil, and serve hot.

AMOUNT PER SERVING NUTRITION FACTS PERCENT DAILY VALUES (based on 2 000 calories)	602 CALORIES 29%	18g PROTEIN 39%	32g FAT 40%	3g FIBER 12%	65g CARBS 50%	0.2g SALT 4%

If you liked this recipe, you will love these as well.

penne with ricotta, zucchini & orange

154

linguine with pesto, potatoes & beans

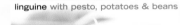

240

pasta with leeks & tomatoes

Scamorza is a hard buffalo or cow's milk cheese similar to mozzarella except that it is smoked. Substitute with provolone if preferred.

Serves 6

20 minutes

35 minutes

2

¼ cup (60 ml) extra-virgin olive oil

2 cloves garlic, finely chopped

2 large leeks, thinly sliced

1½ pounds (750 g) tomatoes, peeled and chopped

Salt and freshly ground black pepper

1 pound (500 g) rigatoni

1 cup (250 g) Scamorza (or other smoked) cheese, diced

Fresh arugula (rocket) leaves, to garnish

1. **Heat** the oil in a large frying pan over medium heat. Add the garlic and sauté 2–3 minutes. Add the leeks and sauté for 5 more minutes.

2. **Add** the tomatoes and season with salt and pepper. Simmer over medium-low heat until reduced, 25–30 minutes.

3. **Meanwhile,** cook the pasta in a large pot of salted boiling water until al dente. Drain well and add to the pan together with the cheese.

4. **Toss gently** over medium heat for 1–2 minutes, garnish with the arugula, and serve hot.

AMOUNT PER SERVING NUTRITION FACTS PERCENT DAILY VALUES (based on 2000 calories)	505 CALORIES 24%	19g PROTEIN 41%	20g FAT 25%	5g FIBER 20%	67g CARBS 52%	0.7g SALT 13%

If you liked this recipe, you will love these as well.

whole-wheat spaghetti with spicy tomato sauce

52

spaghetti with sun-dried tomatoes

262

fusilli with spinach & bell peppers

Shallot-infused white wine adds a mild onion flavor to this dish. You can replace the anchovy paste with 2 mashed anchovy fillets.

 Serves 6

15 minutes

10 minutes

1

1	pound (500 g) fresh spinach leaves, finely shredded
1	red bell pepper (capsicum), seeded and finely chopped
1	yellow bell pepper (capsicum), seeded and finely chopped
1	tablespoon anchovy paste
1	tablespoon water
¼	cup (60 ml) extra-virgin olive oil
1	shallot, finely chopped
2	tablespoons dry white wine
1	pound (500 g) fusilli
1	tablespoon finely chopped thyme

1. **Mix** the spinach, bell peppers, anchovy paste, water, and oil in a large bowl. Toss well.

2. **Wrap** the chopped shallot in a piece of muslin (cheesecloth) and put it in a small bowl with the wine. Let rest for 10 minutes.

3. **Meanwhile,** cook the pasta in a large saucepan of salted boiling water until al dente. Drain well and return to the pot.

4. **Remove** the shallot from the wine and discard it. Drizzle the wine over the pasta and toss gently.

5. **Add** the pasta to the spinach mixture and mix well. Sprinkle with the thyme and serve at once.

AMOUNT PER SERVING	413	14g	12g	5g	66g	0.7g
NUTRITION FACTS	CALORIES	PROTEIN	FAT	FIBER	CARBS	SALT
PERCENT DAILY VALUES (based on 2 000 calories)	20%	30%	15%	20%	51%	13%

If you liked this recipe, you will love these as well.

orecchiette with roasted bell pepper sauce

86

baked penne with bell peppers

210

penne with bell peppers, eggplant & zucchini

126

spirals with beans & pesto

Pesto is made from basil, pine nuts, garlic, and extra-virgin olive oil. These ingredients, combined with the beans and walnuts, make this dish a healthy choice for family meals. Replace the ordinary pasta with whole-wheat pasta, if preferred. Its nutty flavor will blend beautifully with the condiment.

Serves 6

10 minutes

15 minutes

1

PESTO

1	large bunch fresh basil
2	tablespoons pine nuts
2	cloves garlic
½	cup (125 ml) extra-virgin olive oil
	Salt
4	tablespoons freshly grated Parmesan cheese

TO SERVE

5	ounces (150 g) green beans, cut into short lengths
1	pound (500 g) spirals or rotini
1	cup (150 g) frozen peas
1	cup (200 g) canned red kidney beans, drained
½	cup (50 g) chopped walnuts
2	tablespoons extra-virgin olive oil
	Basil leaves, to garnish

1. **To make the pesto,** combine the basil, pine nuts, garlic, oil, and salt in a food processor and chop until smooth. Stir in the cheese. Transfer to a large serving bowl.

2. **Bring** a large pot of salted water to a boil. Add the green beans and return to a boil. Add the pasta and cook for 5 minutes. Add the peas and cook until the pasta is al dente.

3. **Drain** the pasta and vegetables, transfer to a large serving bowl, and toss gently with the pesto. Stir in the kidney beans and walnuts.

4. **Drizzle** with the oil and garnish with the basil leaves. Serve hot.

| AMOUNT PER SERVING **NUTRITION FACTS** PERCENT DAILY VALUES (based on 2 000 calories) | 574 CALORIES 28% | 16g PROTEIN 35% | 31g FAT 38% | 6g FIBER 24% | 63g CARBS 48% | 0.4g SALT 7% |

If you liked this recipe, you will love these as well.

pasta with tomatoes, ricotta & pesto

144

spaghetti with walnut pesto

228

linguine with pesto, potatoes & beans

240

ruote with pesto & cherry tomatoes

The Italian word *ruote* means "wheels." In English, ruote are often called wagonwheel pasta, since they come in the shape of ridged, six-spoke wagon wheels.

Serves 4

15 minutes

20 minutes

1

- ¼ cup (40 g) pine nuts
- ½ cup (75 g) blanched almonds
- 4 cloves garlic
- 1 bunch basil + extra leaves, to garnish
- ⅓ cup (50 g) freshly grated pecorino

Salt and freshly ground black pepper
- ⅓ cup (90 ml) extra-virgin olive oil
- 1 pound (500 g) ruote (wagon wheels)
- 1 pound (500 g) cherry tomatoes, cut in half

1. **Toast** the pine nuts in a large frying pan over medium heat until lightly browned, about 3 minutes. Set aside.

2. **Toast** the almonds in a large frying pan over medium heat until lightly browned, about 3 minutes.

3. **Purée** the garlic and basil in a food processor until smooth. Add the almonds and pecorino and blend until smooth. Season with salt and pepper.

4. **Gradually add** the oil, blending continuously, until the pesto is thick and smooth.

5. **Meanwhile,** cook the pasta in a large pot of salted boiling water until al dente. Drain well, reserving 2 tablespoons of the cooking liquid.

6. **Add** the reserved cooking liquid to the pesto and mix well. Combine the pesto, tomatoes, pine nuts, and pasta in a large serving bowl and toss well. Garnish with basil and serve hot.

AMOUNT PER SERVING	546	16g	28g	4g	62g	1.8g
NUTRITION FACTS	CALORIES	PROTEIN	FAT	FIBER	CARBS	SALT
PERCENT DAILY VALUES (based on 2 000 calories)	26%	35%	35%	16%	48%	32%

If you liked this recipe, you will love these as well.

tagliolini with almond & basil pesto

32

fettuccine with pine nut & walnut pesto

38

spaghetti with walnut pesto

228

penne with ricotta, zucchini & orange

Rich in protein from the ricotta, and brimming with vitamins from the zucchini and orange, this is another healthy, vegetarian dish. Replace the plain pasta with whole-wheat (wholemeal) or spinach pasta, if preferred.

 Serves 6

 10 minutes

20 minutes

1

2	cups (500 g) fresh ricotta cheese, drained
	Finely grated zest and juice of 1 orange
⅓	cup (90 ml) hot water
¼	cup (60 ml) extra-virgin olive oil
	Salt and freshly ground white pepper

1	pound (500 g) penne
3	medium zucchini (courgettes), thinly sliced lengthwise
1	orange, thinly sliced, to garnish

1. **Combine** the ricotta, orange zest and juice, and water in a small bowl. Stir in the oil and season with salt and white pepper.

2. **Cook** the pasta in a large pot of salted boiling water for 5 minutes. Add the zucchini and cook until the pasta is al dente and the zucchini is tender.

3. **Drain well** and transfer to a large bowl. Add the sauce and toss well.

4. **Garnish** with the slices of orange and serve at once.

| AMOUNT PER SERVING **NUTRITION FACTS** PERCENT DAILY VALUES (based on 2000 calories) | 495 CALORIES 24% | 19g PROTEIN 41% | 20g FAT 25% | 3g FIBER 12% | 64g CARBS 49% | 0.2g SALT 4% |

If you liked this recipe, you will love these as well.

grapefruit pasta salad

118

spaghetti with tomato & lemon

254

penne with tomatoes & goat cheese

Capers are the salted or pickled buds of a Mediterranean bush of the same name.
They are widely used in many Mediterranean cuisines, especially that of southern Italy.

 Serves 6

20 minutes

20 minutes

1

1	pound (500 g) penne
1/4	cup (60 ml) extra-virgin olive oil
1	clove garlic, finely chopped
1 1/2	pounds (750 g) cherry tomatoes, halved
12	black olives, pitted

1	tablespoon salt-cured capers, rinsed
	Salt and freshly ground black pepper
1	cup (250 g) fresh, creamy goat cheese
10	leaves fresh basil, torn

1. Cook the pasta in a large pot of salted boiling water until al dente.

2. While the pasta is cooking, heat the oil in a large frying pan over medium heat. Add the garlic and sauté until pale gold, 2–3 minutes.

3. Add the tomatoes, olives, and capers. Season with salt and pepper. Cook over high heat for 5 minutes, stirring frequently.

4. Drain the pasta, reserving 2 tablespoons of the cooking water.

5. Mix the goat cheese with the reserved cooking water in a small bowl.

6. Add the pasta to the pan with the tomatoes, stir in the goat cheese and basil, and toss gently. Serve hot.

AMOUNT PER SERVING NUTRITION FACTS PERCENT DAILY VALUES (based on 2 000 calories)	478 CALORIES 23%	17g PROTEIN 37%	18g FAT 22%	4g FIBER 16%	56g CARBS 43%	0.8g SALT 15%

If you liked this recipe, you will love these as well.

three-cheese penne

170

pasta with goat cheese & artichokes

168

spaghetti with mediterranean pesto

230

pasta with cauliflower

Cauliflower is an excellent source of vitamin K. Be careful not to overcook it; the florets should still be in one piece and slightly firm.

 Serves 6

 20 minutes

 25 minutes

 2

3	tablespoons extra-virgin olive oil	
2	cloves garlic, finely chopped	
1½	pounds (750 g) tomatoes, peeled and chopped	
1	tablespoons finely chopped fresh parsley	

Salt and freshly ground black pepper

1 pound (500 g) rigatoni

1 small cauliflower, broken into florets

6 tablespoons coarsely grated pecorino cheese

1. **Heat** the oil in a large frying pan over medium heat. Add the garlic and sauté until pale gold, 3–4 minutes. Add the tomatoes and parsley. Season with salt and pepper and simmer over low heat for about 20 minutes.

2. **Place** a large pot of lightly salted water over high heat and bring to a boil. Add the pasta and return to a boil. After 7 minutes, add the cauliflower. When the pasta is cooked al dente, drain well.

3. **Transfer** the pasta and cauliflower to the sauce and toss gently. Sprinkle with the pecorino and serve hot.

AMOUNT PER SERVING	414	16g	11g	5g	67g	0.2g
NUTRITION FACTS	CALORIES	PROTEIN	FAT	FIBER	CARBS	SALT
PERCENT DAILY VALUES (based on 2 000 calories)	20%	35%	14%	20%	52%	3%

If you liked this recipe, you will love these as well.

pasta with leeks & tomatoes

146

festonati with italian sausages & broccoli

196

spicy fusilli with swiss chard & pine nuts

Swiss chard leaves should be bright green and fresh looking, with no brown discoloration. Stems should be firm. Unlike many vegetables, larger Swiss chard leaves aren't necessarily tougher than smaller ones.

 Serves 6

 15 minutes

 20 minutes

 1

1 ½ pounds (750 g) Swiss chard (silverbeet), shredded
Salt
¼ cup (60 g) butter
2 cloves garlic, finely sliced
⅓ cup (60 g) pine nuts
1 ½ cups (90 g) fresh bread crumbs

¼ cup (45 g) golden raisins (sultanas)
1 pound (500 g) whole-wheat (wholemeal) or plain fusilli or rotini
1 small, fresh red chile, seeded and sliced

1. **Cook** the Swiss chard in a large pot of lightly salted water until tender, 2–3 minutes. Drain well and place in a bowl of cold water. Drain again, squeezing to remove excess moisture.

2. **Melt** the butter in a large frying pan over medium heat. Add the garlic and sauté until pale golden brown, 3–4 minutes.

3. **Add** the pine nuts and bread crumbs and sauté until golden brown and crisp, about 5 minutes.

4. **Add** the Swiss chard and golden raisins. Mix well and sauté for 2 minutes. Season with salt.

5. **Meanwhile,** cook the pasta in a large pot of salted boiling water until al dente.

6. **Drain well** and add to the pan with the Swiss chard mixture. Add the chile and toss over high heat for 2 minutes. Serve hot.

AMOUNT PER SERVING	464	15g	16g	7g	70g	1.2g
NUTRITION FACTS	CALORIES	PROTEIN	FAT	FIBER	CARBS	SALT
PERCENT DAILY VALUES (based on 2000 calories)	22%	33%	20%	28%	54%	22%

If you liked this recipe, you will love these as well.

homemade spaghetti with garlic & oil

54

bucatini with amatriciana sauce

272

fusilli with ricotta & dried tomatoes

Make your own dried tomatoes by slicing fresh tomatoes and placing them on baking sheets in the oven at its lowest heat for 10–16 hours or until dried, but pliable. Store in airtight jars for up to 6 months.

Serves 6

15 minutes

15 minutes

1

2	cups (500 g) fresh ricotta, drained
1	tablespoon finely chopped fresh mint
1	tablespoon finely chopped fresh parsley
	Salt and freshly ground black pepper
4	ounces (125 g) sun-dried tomatoes, soaked in warm water for 10 minutes, drained, and chopped
1	clove garlic, finely chopped
1	tablespoon salt-cured capers, rinsed
1/3	cup (90 ml) extra-virgin olive oil
3	ounces (150 g) arugula (rocket), chopped + extra leaves, to garnish
1	pound (500 g) fusilli or rotini

1. **Combine** the ricotta, mint, and parsley in a small bowl and beat with a fork to make a smooth cream. Season with salt and pepper.

2. **Put** the tomatoes in a bowl and add the garlic, capers, and oil. Mix well.

3. **Combine** the arugula and tomato mixture in a food processor and chop to make a smooth paste.

4. **Meanwhile**, cook the pasta in a large pot of salted boiling water until al dente. Drain well, reserving 2 tablespoons of the cooking liquid.

5. **Transfer** the pasta to a heated serving bowl. Stir the reserved cooking liquid into the pesto. Add the ricotta and pesto to the pasta and toss well. Garnish with the arugula and serve hot.

AMOUNT PER SERVING NUTRITION FACTS PERCENT DAILY VALUES (based on 2 000 calories)	636 CALORIES 31%	19g PROTEIN 41%	35g FAT 43%	3g FIBER 12%	66g CARBS 51%	0.7g SALT 13%

If you liked this recipe, you will love these as well.

pasta with tomatoes, ricotta & pesto

144

spaghetti with mediterranean pesto

230

penne with gorgonzola

This blue cheese takes its name from the village of Gorgonzola, which lies north of Milan in northern Italy. It has a dense, creamy texture and an irresistible and long-lasting flavor.

 Serves 6

10 minutes

15 minutes

1

¼	cup (60 g) butter
1	cup (250 g) Gorgonzola cheese, crumbled
⅔	cup (150 ml) light (single) cream
1	pound (500 g) penne

½ cup (60 g) freshly grated Parmesan cheese
Salt and freshly ground black pepper
Sprigs of fresh marjoram, to garnish

1. **Heat** the butter and Gorgonzola with the cream in a double boiler over barely simmering water until the cheese has melted, about 5 minutes. Do not stir.

2. **Meanwhile,** cook the penne in a large pot of salted boiling water until al dente. Drain and add to the cheese mixture.

3. **Mix well** so that the pasta is coated with the sauce. Sprinkle with the Parmesan cheese. Season with salt and pepper. Garnish with the marjoram and serve hot.

AMOUNT PER SERVING **NUTRITION FACTS** PERCENT DAILY VALUES (based on 2 000 calories)	600 CALORIES 29%	23g PROTEIN 50%	31g FAT 38%	3g FIBER 12%	63g CARBS 48%	1.1g SALT 20%

If you liked this recipe, you will love these as well.

three-cheese penne
170

spaghetti with ricotta & pecorino
226

whole-wheat spaghetti with gorgonzola
236

pasta with goat cheese & artichokes

In Italy, this recipe is made using caprino, a fresh creamy cheese made from whole or skimmed goat's milk. The name of the cheese derives from the Italian word for goat, *capra*.

Serves 6

15 minutes

25 minutes

2

- 1/3 cup (90 ml) extra-virgin olive oil
- 2 cloves garlic, finely chopped
- 4 fresh artichokes, trimmed and thinly sliced (see page 42 for instructions on how to prepare artichokes)
- 4 tablespoons finely chopped fresh parsley
- 1/4 cup (45 g) pine nuts
- 1 3/4 cups (400 g) soft, creamy goat cheese, such as chèvre
  Salt and freshly ground black pepper
- 1/2 cup (60 g) freshly grated pecorino cheese
- 1 pound (500 g) rigatoni

1. **Heat** 2 tablespoons of oil in a large frying pan over high heat. Add the garlic and sauté for 1 minute. Add the artichokes and sauté until pale golden brown, about 5 minutes.

2. **Lower** the heat, cover, and simmer until tender, about 15 minutes. Add a little water if the pan dries out during simmering. Stir in the parsley.

3. **Toast** the pine nuts in a small frying pan until pale golden brown.

4. **Beat** the goat cheese, pine nuts, salt, pepper, and half the pecorino in a large bowl. Stir in the remaining oil.

5. **Meanwhile,** cook the pasta in a large pot of salted boiling water until al dente. Drain, reserving 2 tablespoons of the cooking liquid.

6. **Add** the pasta and reserved cooking liquid to the goat cheese mixture and toss well. Add the artichoke mixture. Sprinkle with the remaining pecorino, toss well, and serve hot.

AMOUNT PER SERVING	632	24g	34g	3g	63g	1g
NUTRITION FACTS	CALORIES	PROTEIN	FAT	FIBER	CARBS	SALT
PERCENT DAILY VALUES (based on 2000 calories)	30%	52%	42%	12%	48%	17%

If you liked this recipe, you will love these as well.

fettuccine with artichokes

42

bucatini with eggs & artichokes

276

three-cheese penne

Try this dish with whole-wheat (wholemeal) penne. The nutty flavor of the pasta blends in beautifully with the cheeses. If using whole-wheat pasta, garnish with fresh marjoram leaves instead of basil.

 Serves 6

10 minutes

20 minutes

1

1	pound (500 g) penne
1¼	cups (150 g) freshly grated Gruyère cheese
¾	cup (90 g) freshly grated cheddar
⅔	cup (150 g) fresh, creamy goat cheese
½	cup (125 ml) light (single) cream
2	tablespoons snipped fresh chives
	Salt and freshly ground black pepper
	Handful of fresh basil leaves, to garnish

1. **Cook** the penne in a large pot of salted boiling water until al dente. Drain and return to the pan.

2. **Add** all three cheeses, the cream, and chives. Toss gently to combine. Season with salt and pepper.

3. **Spoon** into four to six greased individual baking dishes.

4. **Preheat** a broiler (grill) on high heat. Place the dishes under the broiler until hot and bubbling, 3–5 minutes. Sprinkle with the basil leaves and serve hot.

AMOUNT PER SERVING NUTRITION FACTS PERCENT DAILY VALUES (based on 2 000 calories)	505 CALORIES 24%	22g PROTEIN 48%	20g FAT 25%	2g FIBER 8%	63g CARBS 48%	0.7g SALT 13%

If you liked this recipe, you will love these as well.

penne with gorgonzola

166

spaghetti with ricotta & pecorino

226

whole-wheat spaghetti with gorgonzola

236

cavatappi with shrimp & asparagus

With their slender, spiral shape, cavatappi are an S-shaped pasta tube that resemble a small corkscrew (which is what the name means in Italian). Other pasta varieties that may be substituted include cavatelli, elbow macaroni, and fusilli.

Serves 6

10 minutes

25 minutes

1

¼ cup (60 ml) extra-virgin olive oil

14 ounces (400 g) asparagus trimmed and cut into lengths

2 shallots, finely chopped
Salt and freshly ground black pepper

12 ounces (350 g) shrimp (prawn), shelled and deveined

1 pound (500 g) cavatappi

1. **Heat** 2 tablespoons of oil in a large frying pan over medium heat. Add the asparagus and shallots and sauté over until just tender, 4–5 minutes. Season with salt and pepper.

2. **Heat** the remaining 2 tablespoons of oil in another frying pan over medium-high heat. Add the shrimp and sauté until pink and cooked, 3–5 minutes.

3. **Meanwhile,** cook the pasta in a large pot of salted boiling water until al dente.

4. **Drain well** and add to the pan with the asparagus. Add the shrimp and toss well. Serve hot.

AMOUNT PER SERVING	445 CALORIES	24g PROTEIN	12g FAT	4g FIBER	63g CARBS	0.3g SALT
NUTRITION FACTS PERCENT DAILY VALUES (based on 2000 calories)	21%	52%	15%	16%	48%	5%

If you liked this recipe, you will love these as well.

farfalle with shrimp & pesto

178

penne with tomato & shrimp

186

spaghetti with seafood

298

penne with smoked salmon

Salmon contains high levels of omega-3 fatty acids which are believed to lower the risk of developing heart disease, many types of cancer, Alzheimer's, diabetes, and rheumatoid arthritis.

 Serves 6

 10 minutes

15–20 minutes

 1

2	stalks celery, sliced	5	ounces (150 g) smoked salmon, thinly sliced
2	tomatoes, thinly sliced	2	cloves garlic, whole
1/4	cup (60 ml) white wine vinegar	1	pound (500 g) penne
1/2	cup (125 ml) extra-virgin olive oil	6	tablespoons freshly grated Parmesan cheese
	Salt		

1. **Combine** the celery, tomatoes, vinegar, oil, salt, and smoked salmon in a large serving bowl.

2. **Pierce** the garlic cloves with the tines (prongs) of a fork and use it to stir the ingredients in the bowl. The garlic will flavor the mixture (take care that the cloves do not come off).

3. **Meanwhile,** cook the penne in a large saucepan of salted boiling water until al dente.

4. **Drain well** and transfer to the bowl with the salmon mixture. Add the Parmesan and toss gently. Serve hot or at room temperature.

AMOUNT PER SERVING	468	16g	20g	3g	59g	1.1g
NUTRITION FACTS	**CALORIES**	**PROTEIN**	**FAT**	**FIBER**	**CARBS**	**SALT**
PERCENT DAILY VALUES (based on 2 000 calories)	22%	35%	25%	15%	45%	20%

If you liked this recipe, you will love these as well.

fettuccine with salmon & peas

64

salmon ravioli with lemon & dill

92

spaghetti with vodka & caviar

300

penne with seafood & orange

Imitation crab sticks are processed seafood made from finely pulverized white fish flesh shaped and cured to resemble snow crab legs.

 Serves 6

 15 minutes

 20 minutes

 1

16   fresh or frozen imitation crab sticks
⅓   cup (90 ml) extra-virgin olive oil
2   cloves garlic, finely chopped
2   tablespoons finely chopped fresh parsley
1   tablespoon orange zest, cut in julienne strips

⅓   cup (90 ml) cognac
½   cup (125 ml) freshly squeezed orange juice
    Salt and freshly ground black pepper
½   cup (125 ml) heavy (double) cream
1   pound (500 g) penne

1. **Coarsely chop** the crab sticks.

2. **Pour** the oil into a large frying pan over medium heat. Add the garlic and parsley and sauté for 1 minute.

3. **Add** the crab sticks and orange zest. Mix well and sauté for 1 minute. Pour in the cognac and cook until it has evaporated. Add the orange juice. Season with salt and a generous grinding of pepper.

4. **Simmer** over low heat until the liquid has evaporated, about 5 minutes, then add the cream.

5. **Meanwhile,** cook the pasta in a large pot of salted boiling water until al dente.

6. **Drain well** and transfer to the pan with the sauce. Toss gently for 1–2 minutes. Serve immediately.

AMOUNT PER SERVING	558 CALORIES	15g PROTEIN	26g FAT	3g FIBER	67g CARBS	0.8g SALT
NUTRITION FACTS PERCENT DAILY VALUES (based on 2 000 calories)	27%	33%	32%	12%	52%	14%

If you liked this recipe, you will love these as well.

penne with smoked salmon

174

spaghetti with lobster

296

farfalle with shrimp & pesto

Shrimp is an excellent source of protein, selenium, and vitamin B12. To remove the shrimp's intestine (devein) before cooking, make a shallow incision along the underside of the shrimp and pull out the dark vein that runs its length.

Serves 6

10 minutes

40 minutes

1

½ cup (90 g) pine nuts

5 cups (250 g) arugula (rocket)

⅓ cup (90 ml) extra-virgin olive oil

2 cloves garlic, finely chopped

½ cup (60 g) freshly grated Parmesan cheese

Salt and freshly ground black pepper

8 ounces (250 g) shrimp (prawn) tails, shelled and deveined

1 pound (500 g) farfalle

1. Put the pine nuts in a large frying pan over medium heat. Do not add any cooking oil or fat. Toast, shaking the pan often, until golden brown, about 5 minutes.

2. Chop the arugula and toasted pine nuts in a food processor with 5 tablespoons of the oil, garlic, and Parmesan until smooth. Season with salt and pepper.

3. Heat the remaining 1 tablespoon of oil in a large frying pan over high heat.

Add the shrimp and sauté until pink and cooked through, 3–4 minutes. Season with salt and pepper.

4. Meanwhile, cook the pasta in a large pot of salted boiling water until al dente.

5. Drain the pasta and add to the frying pan with the shrimp. Add the arugula pesto and toss gently over medium-high heat for 1–2 minutes. Serve hot.

AMOUNT PER SERVING NUTRITION FACTS PERCENT DAILY VALUES (based on 2000 calories)	600 CALORIES 29%	25g PROTEIN 54%	29g FAT 36%	3g FIBER 12%	64g CARBS 49%	0.4g SALT 7%

If you liked this recipe, you will love these as well.

fettuccine with scallops

60

spaghetti with clams, chile & arugula

290

whole-wheat penne with tuna, avocado & fresh herbs

Whole-wheat pasta has more dietary fiber than standard pasta. It also contains more vitamins, especially B vitamins, and keeps you feeling full for longer since it is digested slowly.

Serves 6

30 minutes

10–12 minutes

1

1	small bunch fresh parsley
1	small bunch fresh basil
1	small bunch fresh dill
⅓	cup (90 ml) extra-virgin olive oil
	Salt
2	scallions (spring onions), thinly sliced
1	large red bell pepper (capsicum), cut in small dice
1	avocado, peeled, pitted, and sliced
	Freshly squeezed juice of 1 lemon
5	ounces (150 g) canned tuna, packed in oil, drained
1	pound (500 g) whole-wheat (wholemeal) penne
	Salt and freshly ground black pepper

1. **Chop** the parsley, basil, and dill in a food processor with 4 tablespoons of oil and a pinch of salt. Chop until smooth. Put in a large serving bowl.

2. **Put** the scallions and bell pepper in a separate bowl. Drizzle the avocado with the lemon juice (to stop it from turning black), and put in the bowl with the bell pepper mixture.

3. **Crumble** the tuna and put in another bowl.

4. **Meanwhile,** cook the pasta in a large pot of salted boiling water until al dente.

5. **Drain well** and add to the bowl with the creamed herbs.

6. **Add** the bell pepper mixture and tuna. Toss quickly, drizzle with the remaining oil, and season with salt and pepper. Serve immediately.

AMOUNT PER SERVING	495	19g	23g	9g	58g	0.4g
NUTRITION FACTS	**CALORIES**	**PROTEIN**	**FAT**	**FIBER**	**CARBS**	**SALT**
PERCENT DAILY VALUES (based on 2 000 calories)	24%	41%	28%	36%	45%	8%

If you liked this recipe, you will love these as well.

farfalle with yogurt sauce & avocado

142

spaghetti with yogurt & avocado

238

pasta with tuna sauce

Really fresh tuna is deep red—almost maroon—and is plump and absolutely firm to the touch.

Serves 6

20 minutes

70 minutes

2

- ¼ cup (60 ml) extra-virgin olive oil
- 2 onions, chopped
- 4 cloves garlic, lightly crushed but whole
- ⅔ cup (150 ml) dry white wine
- 1¼ pounds (600 g) peeled plum tomatoes, pressed through a fine-mesh strainer (passata)
- 1 pound (500 g) fresh tuna, skin removed

- 1 small bunch fennel leaves, finely chopped, and/or 1 tablespoon finely chopped fresh mint
  Salt and freshly ground black pepper
  Fish stock or water (optional)
- 1 pound (500 g) rigatoni
- ½ cup (125 g) freshly grated ricotta salata cheese

1. **Heat** the oil in a large saucepan over a low heat and sauté the onions and garlic for about 10 minutes, or until the onion has softened.

2. **Pour in** the wine and add the tomatoes, tuna, fennel, and/or the mint. Season with salt and pepper and bring to a boil.

3. **Lower** the heat and simmer, partially covered, for at least 1 hour, adding fish stock or hot water if the sauce begins to stick to the pan.

4. **Remove** the tuna and crumble coarsely with a fork. Return the tuna meat to the sauce.

5. **Cook** the pasta in a large pot of salted boiling water for 3–4 minutes, or until al dente. Drain and serve with the tuna sauce. Sprinkle with the cheese and serve hot.

AMOUNT PER SERVING	560	33g	17g	4g	70g	0.2g
NUTRITION FACTS	CALORIES	PROTEIN	FAT	FIBER	CARBS	SALT
PERCENT DAILY VALUES (based on 2 000 calories)	27%	72%	21%	16%	54%	4%

If you liked this recipe, you will love these as well.

pasta salad with tuna & olives

128

spaghetti with tuna & capers

286

fusilli with fish cakes

If desired, add 12–16 halved raw cherry tomatoes along with the chile and fish cakes at the end.

 Serves 6

 20 minutes

15 minutes

 2

1	large bread roll
3	tablespoons milk
14	ounces (400 g) white fish fillets (hake, cod, whiting, dogfish, rockfish, ocean perch, red snapper), boned and skin removed
1	large egg
3	tablespoons freshly grated Parmesan cheese
1	tablespoon finely chopped fresh parsley

	Salt and freshly ground black pepper
3	tablespoons all-purpose (plain) flour
½	cup (125 ml) extra-virgin olive oil
1	pound (500 g) fusilli or rotini
1	fresh red chile, seeded and finely chopped
2	tablespoons finely chopped fresh dill

1. To make the fish cakes, put the bread in the bowl of a food processor. Drizzle with the milk and blend for a few seconds.

2. Add the fish and blend for a few seconds more. Add the egg, Parmesan, and parsley. Season with salt and pepper. Blend until smooth.

3. Shape the mixture into marble-sized balls. Flour a clean work surface and roll the balls in the flour, shaking off the excess.

4. Heat ⅓ cup (90 ml) of oil in a large frying pan over medium heat. Fry the fish cakes until lightly browned, 4–5 minutes. Drain well on paper towels.

5. Meanwhile, cook the pasta in a large pot of salted boiling water until al dente. Drain and drizzle with the remaining oil.

6. Put in a large heated serving bowl and add the fish cakes and chile. Toss gently. Sprinkle with the dill and serve.

AMOUNT PER SERVING	603	27g	24g	3g	75g	0.4g
NUTRITION FACTS	CALORIES	PROTEIN	FAT	FIBER	CARBS	SALT
PERCENT DAILY VALUES (based on 2000 calories)	29%	59%	30%	12%	58%	7%

If you liked this recipe, you will love these as well.

pappardelle marinara

66

penne with tomato & shrimp

186

penne with tomato & shrimp

If you have raw shrimp, peel and devein them, then sauté in a little hot oil over medium-high heat until they turn pink.

 Serves 6

 10 minutes

 10–15 minutes

 1

1	pound (500 g) penne
1/3	cup (90 ml) extra-virgin olive oil
4	cloves garlic, lightly crushed but whole
4	scallions (spring onions), finely chopped
20	leaves fresh basil

	Salt
1	pound (500 g) mixed large and small shrimp (prawns), peeled and cooked
4	large tomatoes, peeled and chopped
1	pound (500 g) cherry tomatoes, halved

1. **Cook** the pasta in a large pot of salted boiling water until al dente.

2. **While the pasta is cooking,** heat the oil in a small pan over low heat. Add the garlic, scallions, and basil and sauté until the garlic turns pale gold, 3–4 minutes.

3. **Transfer** the mixture to a food processor and blend until smooth. Season with salt.

4. **Put** the cooked shrimp in a large bowl. Add the garlic mixture and mix well.

5. **Drain** the pasta and add to the bowl with the shrimp.

6. **Stir** the chopped tomatoes and cherry tomatoes into the pasta, tossing well. Serve at once.

AMOUNT PER SERVING	524	28g	17g	4g	67g	0.4g
NUTRITION FACTS	CALORIES	PROTEIN	FAT	FIBER	CARBS	SALT
PERCENT DAILY VALUES (based on 2 000 calories)	25%	6%	21%	16%	52%	8%

If you liked this recipe, you will love these as well.

penne with swordfish & salmon

188

penne with mussels

190

seafood spaghetti en papillote

302

penne with swordfish & salmon

The swordfish and salmon in this dish not only provide lots of flavor, they are also rich in protein and essential omega-3 fatty acids.

 Serves 6

15 minutes

35 minutes

 1

1	pound (500 g) penne
¼	cup (60 ml) extra-virgin olive oil
1	clove garlic, finely chopped
1	small onion, finely chopped
4	ounces (125 g) swordfish, cut into bite-size chunks
4	ounces (125 g) salmon, cut into bite-size chunks
⅓	cup (90 ml) dry white wine
14	ounces (400 g) cherry tomatoes, halved
2	tablespoons finely chopped fresh parsley
	Salt

1. **Cook** the pasta in a large pot of salted boiling water until al dente.

2. **While the pasta is cooking,** heat the oil in a large frying pan over medium heat. Add the garlic and onion and sauté until softened, about 5 minutes.

3. **Add** the swordfish and salmon. Sauté for 3 minutes. Add the wine and simmer until it evaporates. Remove the fish and set aside.

4. **Add** the tomatoes and simmer over medium-low heat for 5 minutes.

5. **Return** the fish to the pan. Add the parsley and season with salt.

6. **Drain** the pasta and add to the sauce. Toss gently over high heat for 1 minute. Serve hot.

AMOUNT PER SERVING **NUTRITION FACTS** PERCENT DAILY VALUES (based on 2000 calories)	368 CALORIES 18%	19g PROTEIN 41%	5g FAT 6%	3g FIBER 12%	64g CARBS 49%	0.1g SALT 2%

If you liked this recipe, you will love these as well.

pappardelle marinara

66

pasta with tuna sauce

182

spaghetti with vodka & caviar

300

penne with mussels

Shop around when buying mussels and select those with tightly closed shells, avoiding any that are broken. Always eat mussels on the same day that you buy them.

Serves 6

15 minutes

1 hour

20–30 minutes

2

2	pounds (1 kg) fresh mussels, in shell
1/4	cup (60 ml) extra-virgin olive oil
2	cloves garlic, finely chopped
1	pound (500 g) penne
10	cups (2.5 liters) vegetable stock (homemade or from bouillon cubes), boiling + extra, as required

1	pound (500 g) potatoes, peeled and cut into 1/2-inch (1-cm) cubes
1	pound (500 g) cherry tomatoes, halved
	Leaves from 1 sprig of basil, torn + extra, to garnish
	Salt and freshly ground black pepper

1. **Soak** the mussels in a large bowl of cold water for 1 hour. Rinse well and scrub or pull off the beards.

2. **Heat** 2 tablespoons of the oil in a large saucepan over medium heat. Add the garlic and sauté until pale golden brown, 3–4 minutes.

3. **Add** the mussels and cook over medium-high heat until they open, 7–10 minutes. Remove from the heat. Shell the mussels, discarding any that did not open.

4. **Filter** the cooking juices through a piece of muslin (cheesecloth) and set aside.

5. **Heat** the remaining oil in a large saucepan over medium heat. Add the pasta and mix well. Sauté for 2 minutes and then add the cooking juices from the mussels and the stock.

6. **Cover** and simmer over low heat for 5 minutes. Add the potatoes and simmer for 5 minutes. Add the tomatoes and simmer until the pasta is al dente and the potatoes are tender, 5–10 minutes.

7. **Drain well** and transfer to a heated serving bowl. Add the mussels and basil, and season with salt and pepper. Toss well. Garnish with the basil and serve hot.

AMOUNT PER SERVING	CALORIES	PROTEIN	FAT	FIBER	CARBS	SALT
NUTRITION FACTS	490	20g	12g	4g	80g	0.4g
PERCENT DAILY VALUES (based on 2 000 calories)	24%	43%	15%	16%	62%	8%

sedani with bacon & peas

Sedani are a smooth short pasta. Substitute with penne, fusilli, or farfalle (bow ties), if preferred. This recipe is also good when made with whole-wheat (wholemeal) pasta.

 Serves 6

 15 minutes

15 minutes

 1

2	tablespoons extra-virgin olive oil
1	shallot, finely chopped
5	ounces (150 g) thinly sliced bacon, rinds removed, chopped
½	cup (125 ml) dry white wine
1	cup (150 g) frozen peas
	Salt and freshly ground black pepper

1	pound (500 g) sedani or penne
1	cup (125 g) coarsely grated pecorino cheese
2	tablespoons snipped fresh chives

1. **Heat** the oil in a large frying pan over medium heat. Add the shallot and sauté until transparent, 2–3 minutes.

2. **Add** the bacon and sauté until crisp and golden brown, 3–4 minutes.

3. **Pour** in the wine and add the peas. Season with salt and pepper. Simmer over low heat until the wine has evaporated and the peas are tender, about 5 minutes.

4. **Meanwhile,** cook the pasta in a large pot of salted boiling water until al dente.

5. **Drain well** and add to pan with the bacon and pea mixture. Add the cheese and chives and toss gently over low heat for 1–2 minutes. Serve hot.

AMOUNT PER SERVING **NUTRITION FACTS** PERCENT DAILY VALUES (based on 2 000 calories)	487 CALORIES 23%	23g PROTEIN 50%	16g FAT 20%	4g FIBER 16%	64g CARBS 49%	1.3g SALT 24%

If you liked this recipe, you will love these as well.

farfalle with peas & ham

198

penne with peas & sausage

204

spicy spaghetti with pancetta & onion

278

penne with zucchini, ham & pistachios

To blanch the pistachios, remove the nuts from their shells. Plunge them into a small saucepan of boiling water for 1 minute. Drain and remove any loose skins.

 Serves 6

 15 minutes

20 minutes

1

- ¼ cup (60 ml) extra-virgin olive oil
- 8 scallions (spring onions), white and green parts sliced separately
- ⅓ cup (90 ml) dry white wine
- 8 small zucchini (courgettes), cut into small cubes
  Salt
- 8 ounces (250 g) smoked ham, cut into small cubes

- ⅔ cup (100 g) blanched pistachios, coarsely chopped
  Freshly ground black pepper
- 1 pound (500 g) penne
- 3 tablespoons butter
- ½ cup (60 g) freshly grated Parmesan cheese

1. Heat the oil in a large frying pan over medium heat. Add the white part of the scallions. Sauté until they begin to soften, about 2 minutes. Add the wine and let evaporate for 3 minutes.

2. Add the zucchini and season with salt. Mix well and sauté until the zucchini are tender, about 5 minutes.

3. Add the ham, pistachios, and half the green part of the scallions. Mix well and sauté for 1 minute. Season with pepper.

4. Meanwhile, cook the pasta in a large pot of salted boiling water until al dente. Drain well and add to the pan with the sauce. Toss over high heat for 1 minute.

5. Add the butter and Parmesan and toss well. Sprinkle with the remaining scallions and serve hot.

AMOUNT PER SERVING	627	27g	29g	4g	65g	1.5g
NUTRITION FACTS	**CALORIES**	**PROTEIN**	**FAT**	**FIBER**	**CARBS**	**SALT**
PERCENT DAILY VALUES (based on 2000 calories)	30%	59%	36%	16%	50%	28%

If you liked this recipe, you will love these as well.

penne with raw zucchini, pecorino & mint

134

penne with bell peppers, eggplant & zucchini

126

spaghetti with zucchini

246

farfalle with peas & ham

Use a fresh, high-fat heavy (double) cream in this dish. Light (single) cream may be healthier but anything with butterfat under 35 percent is more likely to curdle during cooking.

 Serves 6

10 minutes

15–20 minutes

1

¼	cup (60 g) butter
1¾	cups (250 g) fresh or frozen peas
8	ounces (250 g) ham, thinly sliced and cut in small squares
¼	cup (60 ml) heavy (double) cream

Salt and freshly ground black pepper

1	pound (500 g) farfalle
2	tablespoons finely chopped fresh parsley
½	cup (60 g) freshly grated Parmesan cheese

1. Heat the butter in a large frying pan over medium-low heat. Add the peas and ham and sauté until the peas are tender, 5–10 minutes.

2. Stir in 2 tablespoons of the cream and simmer until the sauce thickens. Season with salt and pepper.

3. Meanwhile, cook the farfalle in a large pot of salted boiling water until al dente.

4. Drain well and transfer to the pan with the sauce. Add the remaining 2 tablespoons of cream, parsley, and Parmesan. Toss well and serve hot.

AMOUNT PER SERVING	521	24g	30g	5g	66g	1.5g
NUTRITION FACTS	CALORIES	PROTEIN	FAT	FIBER	CARBS	SALT
PERCENT DAILY VALUES (based on 2 000 calories)	25%	52%	37%	20%	51%	28%

If you liked this recipe, you will love these as well.

sedani with bacon & peas

192

penne with peas & sausage

204

maccheroni with tomatoes & smoked ham

In Italy, this recipe is made using speck, a type of smoked ham with a salty flavor from Tyrol.

 Serves 6

 10 minutes

 20 minutes

 1

¼ cup (60 ml) extra-virgin olive oil

2 shallots, finely chopped

2 pounds (1 kg) ripe tomatoes, peeled and chopped

2 teaspoons fennel seeds

1 tablespoon torn basil + extra to garnish

1 cup (125 g) diced smoked ham or bacon

Salt and freshly ground black pepper

1 pound (500 g) maccheroni (macaroni)

6 tablespoons freshly grated Parmesan cheese

1. **Place** the oil in a large frying pan over medium heat. Add the shallots and sauté until softened, 3–4 minutes.

2. **Stir in** the tomatoes, fennel seeds, and basil. Simmer until the tomatoes begin to break down, about 10 minutes. Add the speck and simmer for 5 minutes. Season with salt and pepper.

3. **Meanwhile,** cook the pasta in a large pot of salted boiling water until al dente. Drain and add to the sauce.

4. **Toss** over high heat for 1 minute. Sprinkle with the Parmesan and garnish with the basil. Serve hot.

AMOUNT PER SERVING NUTRITION FACTS PERCENT DAILY VALUES (based on 2 000 calories)	470 CALORIES 23%	18g PROTEIN 39%	17g FAT 21%	4g FIBER 16%	66g CARBS 51%	1g SALT 17%

If you liked this recipe, you will love these as well.

pasta squares with tomato & pancetta

34

bucatini with amatriciana sauce

272

garganelli with creamy sausage sauce

Garganelli are a curly pasta from the Emilia-Romagna region of Italy. They are traditionally served with thick, meaty sauces like this one. Substitute with penne, if preferred.

 Serves 6

15 minutes

15 minutes

1

1	tablespoon butter
1	onion, finely chopped
1	pound (500 g) Italian pork sausage, crumbled
¾	cup (180 ml) light (single) cream
¼	teaspoon freshly grated nutmeg

	Salt and freshly ground black pepper
1	pound (500 g) garganelli or penne
½	cup (60 g) freshly grated Parmesan cheese
1	tablespoon finely chopped fresh parsley

1. **Heat** the butter in a large frying pan over medium heat. Add the onion and sauté until softened, about 5 minutes.

2. **Add** the sausage and sauté over high heat until browned all over, about 3 minutes.

3. **Pour in** the cream and simmer over very low heat for about 10 minutes. Season with nutmeg, salt, and pepper.

4. **Meanwhile,** cook the pasta in a large pot of salted boiling water until al dente. Drain and add to the sauce.

5. **Sprinkle** with the Parmesan and parsley and toss gently. Serve hot.

AMOUNT PER SERVING	631	24g	29g	4g	72g	2g
NUTRITION FACTS	**CALORIES**	**PROTEIN**	**FAT**	**FIBER**	**CARBS**	**SALT**
PERCENT DAILY VALUES (based on 2 000 calories)	30%	52%	36%	16%	52%	36%

If you liked this recipe, you will love these as well.

pappardelle with sausage & mushrooms

68

festonati with italian sausages & broccoli

196

spaghetti with italian sausage sauce

308

penne with peas & sausage

Use ridged penne for this dish. This style of pasta is perfect for holding thick, creamy sauces.

 Serves 6

 15 minutes

 20 minutes

 1

2	tablespoons butter
1	onion, finely chopped
2	tablespoons unseasoned tomato sauce, store-bought or homemade
1	pound (500 g) Italian sausage, crumbled
5	tablespoons (75 ml) light (single) cream
2	tablespoons extra-virgin olive oil
1	clove garlic, finely chopped
1	small bunch fresh sage, finely chopped

2	cups (300 g) frozen peas
	Pinch of sugar
1	cup (250 ml) hot water, + more as needed
	Salt and freshly ground black pepper
2	tablespoons finely chopped fresh parsley
1	pound (500 g) penne
½	cup (60 g) freshly grated Parmesan cheese

1. Heat the butter in a medium saucepan over a medium heat. Add the onion and sauté until softened, 4–5 minutes.

2. Stir in the tomato sauce and sausage. Pour in the cream and simmer over a low heat for 15 minutes.

3. Heat the oil in a medium saucepan over low heat, add the garlic and sage and sauté for about 3 minutes or until the garlic is pale gold.

4. Stir in the peas, sugar, and water. Simmer for about 10 minutes or until the peas are tender. Season with salt and pepper and add the parsley.

5. Meanwhile, cook the pasta in a large pot of salted boiling water until al dente. Drain the pasta and add to the sauce together with the cream and sausage mixture. Toss well. Sprinkle with the Parmesan and serve hot.

AMOUNT PER SERVING	695	26g	35g	5g	75g	1.8g
NUTRITION FACTS	CALORIES	PROTEIN	FAT	FIBER	CARBS	SALT
PERCENT DAILY VALUES (based on 2 000 calories)	33%	57%	43%	20%	58%	34%

If you liked this recipe, you will love these as well.

whole-wheat penne with tuna, avocado & fresh herbs

180

farfalle with peas & ham

198

garganelli with creamy sausage sauce

202

sedani with meatballs

With prosciutto (Parma ham), ground beef, garlic, and parsley, these meatballs make a substantial, warming dish on a cold, wintry day.

Serves 6

45 minutes

30 minutes

2

- 1/3 cup (90 ml) milk
- 2 thick slices day-old bread, crusts removed, crumbled
- 1 pound (500 g) ground (minced) beef
- 4 ounces (125 g) prosciutto (Parma ham)
  Small bunch fresh parsley
- 1 clove garlic
- 1 large egg yolk
  Finely grated zest of 1 lemon
  Pinch of nutmeg

Salt and freshly ground black pepper
- 1/2 cup (75 g) all-purpose (plain) flour + extra, to dust
- 5 tablespoons extra-virgin olive oil
- 1 small onion, finely chopped
- 2 pounds (1 kg) tomatoes, peeled and chopped
- 1 teaspoon dried oregano
- 1 pound (500 g) sedani
- 1/2 cup (60 g) freshly grated Parmesan cheese

1. Pour the milk into a small bowl and add the bread.

2. Put the beef, prosciutto, parsley, and garlic in a food processor and chop until smooth. Transfer to a bowl and add the well-squeezed bread, egg yolk, lemon zest, and nutmeg. Season with salt and pepper and mix well.

3. Dust a work surface with flour. Shape the mixture into balls about the size of a marble and roll in the flour. Set aside.

4. Heat the oil in a large frying pan and sauté the onion until translucent, 3–4 minutes. Add the tomatoes and

oregano and simmer over medium heat for 10–15 minutes. Season with salt and pepper.

5. Cook the meatballs in a medium pan of simmering water for 3 minutes. Scoop out with a slotted spoon and drain on a clean cloth.

6. Cook the pasta in a large pot of salted boiling water until al dente.

7. Drain and add to the pan with the tomato sauce. Add the meatballs and toss gently over medium heat for 1–2 minutes. Sprinkle with the Parmesan and serve hot.

AMOUNT PER SERVING NUTRITION FACTS PERCENT DAILY VALUES (based on 2000 calories)	CALORIES	PROTEIN	FAT	FIBER	CARBS	SALT
	741	39g	30g	6g	84g	1.6g
	36%	85%	37%	24%	65%	28%

penne with meat sauce

If you have time, simmer this sauce over low heat for 2–3 hours. Add more stock as it reduces. The longer you cook the sauce, the tastier it will become.

 Serves 6

 15 minutes

 1 hour 30 minutes

 1

MEAT SAUCE

2	tablespoons butter
1	carrot, finely chopped
2	stalks celery, finely chopped
1	medium onion, finely chopped
1	pound (500 g) ground (minced) pork
5	ounces (150 g) ground (minced) beef
1	cup (120 g) diced ham
²⁄₃	cup (150 ml) dry white wine

6	large tomatoes, peeled and coarsely chopped
	Salt and freshly ground black pepper
¼	teaspoon freshly ground nutmeg
¾	cup (180 ml) beef stock (homemade or from bouillon cube)
1	pound (500 g) penne
½	cup (60 g) freshly grated Parmesan cheese

1. **To prepare the meat sauce,** heat the butter in a large frying pan over medium heat. Add the carrot, celery, and onion and sauté until softened, about 5 minutes.

2. **Add** the pork and beef and sauté until browned, 5–7 minutes. Add the ham and cook for 1 minute. Increase the heat to high, pour in the wine, and let it evaporate for about 5 minutes.

3. **Stir in** the tomatoes. Season with salt, pepper, and nutmeg. Partially cover the pan and simmer over low heat for at least 1 hour. Add the stock gradually during cooking to keep the sauce moist.

4. **Cook** the pasta in a large pot of salted boiling water until al dente. Drain well and add to the sauce. Sprinkle with the Parmesan and toss well. Serve hot.

AMOUNT PER SERVING	571 CALORIES	37g PROTEIN	19g FAT	4g FIBER	63g CARBS	1.1g SALT
NUTRITION FACTS PERCENT DAILY VALUES (based on 2000 calories)	27%	80%	23%	16%	48%	21%

If you liked this recipe, you will love these as well.

fettuccine roman style
76

pappardelle with meat sauce
78

lasagna with meatballs
108

baked penne with bell peppers

Penne are among the most common short pasta shapes. There are two types: ridged and smooth. The ridged type holds chunky sauces better than the smooth one.

Serves 6

35 minutes

45 minutes

2

1½	pounds (750 g) red and yellow bell peppers (capsicums), halved and seeded
1	pound (500 g) penne
¼	cup (60 ml) extra-virgin olive oil
2	cloves garlic, lightly crushed but whole
¼	cup (50 g) salt-cured capers, rinsed
½	cup (50 g) black olives, pitted and coarsely chopped
2	tablespoons finely chopped fresh parsley
2	tablespoons fine dry bread crumbs
	Salt and freshly ground black pepper
1	tablespoon finely chopped fresh oregano
1¼	cups (150 g) freshly grated Parmesan cheese

1. **Broil (grill)** the bell peppers on a high heat, turning them often, until the skins are blackened. Wrap in a brown paper bag for 10 minutes. Take out of the bag and remove the skins. Clean carefully with paper towels and cut into thin strips.

2. **Cook** the pasta in a large saucepan of salted boiling water until not quite al dente.

3. **Meanwhile,** heat the oil in a large frying pan over a medium heat and sauté 1 clove of garlic for 2–3 minutes or until pale gold. Remove from the heat.

4. **Finely chop** the remaining garlic and add to the pan with the capers, olives, bell peppers, parsley, and bread crumbs. Season with salt and pepper.

5. **Cook** over a low heat for 10 minutes, stirring occasionally. Add the oregano and remove from the heat.

6. **Preheat** the oven to 425°F (220°C/ gas 7). Butter a baking dish.

7. **Drain** the pasta and add half the bell pepper mixture. Spoon the mixture into the prepared baking dish, cover with the remaining bell pepper mixture, and sprinkle with the Parmesan.

8. **Bake** for about 15 minutes, or until lightly browned and crisp on top. Serve hot.

AMOUNT PER SERVING						
NUTRITION FACTS	560	22g	20g	5g	79g	1.1g
PERCENT DAILY VALUES (based on 2000 calories)	CALORIES	PROTEIN	FAT	FIBER	CARBS	SALT
	27%	48%	25%	20%	61%	20%

spinach-stuffed pasta shells
with tomato sauce

The conchiglioni shells are stuffed with onion, cheese, basil, and garlic and sit on a light tomato sauce. This is an impressive dish for a special occasion.

Serves 6

40 minutes

70 minutes

3

30	jumbo conchiglioni pasta shells (jumbo shells)
14	ounces (400 g) frozen chopped spinach, thawed
1	large handful of fresh baby spinach leaves
1	small Spanish onion, finely chopped
1¾	cups (400 g) ricotta cheese
1	cup (125 g) freshly grated Parmesan cheese + extra, to serve
2	tablespoons fennel seeds

20	fresh basil leaves, chopped
3	garlic cloves, finely chopped
	Salt and freshly ground black pepper
1	tablespoon extra-virgin olive oil
6	scallions (spring onions), chopped
3	pounds (1.5 kg) tomatoes, coarsely chopped
1	tablespoon sugar
2	tablespoons finely chopped fresh dill

1. Preheat the oven to 350°F (180°C/gas 4).

2. Cook the pasta shells in a large saucepan of salted boiling water until al dente, then drain and allow them to cool.

3. Squeeze the defrosted spinach dry and transfer to a large bowl. Quickly blanch the baby spinach leaves in hot water, then drain and add to the defrosted spinach.

4. Add the onion, ricotta, grated Parmesan, fennel, basil and garlic and mix thoroughly. Add salt and pepper.

5. Heat the oil in a deep pan and add the chopped scallions. Sauté for 2 minutes, then add the chopped tomatoes, sugar,

salt and pepper, and simmer for 30 minutes.

6. Add the dill, stirring thoroughly, then season with salt and pepper if necessary. Set aside.

7. Spoon the spinach mixture into the pasta shells, adding just enough to fill each shell. Set aside.

8. Divide the tomato sauce among six ovenproof dishes and place the filled pasta-shells on top of the sauce in each dish.

9. Sprinkle with the extra Parmesan cheese, cover the dishes with foil and bake for 20 minutes. Remove the foil and bake for another 5 minutes or until golden.

AMOUNT PER SERVING	548	29g	19g	7g	73g	0.6g
NUTRITION FACTS	**CALORIES**	**PROTEIN**	**FAT**	**FIBER**	**CARBS**	**SALT**
PERCENT DAILY VALUES (based on 2000 calories)	26%	63%	23%	28%	56%	11%

spinach & ricotta cannelloni
with tomato sauce

This baked cannelloni dish is fairly filling and can be served as a one-dish meal.

 Serves 4

20 minutes

40 minutes

1

2	pounds (1 kg) fresh spinach leaves, tough stems removed
1½	cups (375 g) ricotta cheese, drained
2	teaspoons freshly grated nutmeg
12	dried cannelloni tubes
3	cups (750 g) peeled plum tomatoes, pressed through a fine-mesh strainer (passata)

1. **Preheat** the oven to 350°F (180°C/gas 4).

2. **Cook** the spinach in a large saucepan of boiling water for 1 minute. Drain well.

3. **Coarsely chop** the spinach and place in a large bowl. Mix in the ricotta and nutmeg until well combined.

4. **Using a pastry bag** fitted with a medium tip, fill the cannelloni tubes with the spinach and ricotta mixture.

5. **Arrange** the filled cannelloni in a shallow baking dish and pour the tomatoes over the top.

6. **Bake,** uncovered, for about 40 minutes, or until the pasta is al dente. Serve hot.

AMOUNT PER SERVING	478	25g	13g	8g	72g	1g
NUTRITION FACTS	**CALORIES**	**PROTEIN**	**FAT**	**FIBER**	**CARBS**	**SALT**
PERCENT DAILY VALUES (based on 2000 calories)	23%	54%	16%	32%	55%	19%

If you liked this recipe, you will love these as well.

spinach-stuffed pasta shells with tomato sauce

202

baked pasta & vegetables

216

baked pasta & vegetables

This hearty vegetarian dish comes from southern Italy, where pasta and vegetable bakes are common fare. If you are using fresh tomatoes, make sure that they are plump and filled with juice.

Serves 6

10 minutes

1 hour

2

½	cup (125 ml) extra-virgin olive oil
3	pounds (1.5 kg) juicy, ripe tomatoes or 4 cups (400 g) canned Italian tomatoes, with juice
	Handful of fresh basil leaves
1	pound (500 g) small penne
1	pound (500 g) potatoes, peeled and cut into ¼-inch (5mm) slices
2½	cups (250 g) black olives, pitted and sliced

1	large onion, sliced
1	tablespoon finely chopped fresh oregano
	Salt and freshly ground black pepper
1	cup (120 g) freshly grated pecorino or Parmesan cheese
½	cup (60 g) fine dry bread crumbs
4	tablespoons pine nuts

1. Preheat the oven to 350°F (180°C/gas 4).

2. Grease a large deep baking dish with 2 tablespoons of the oil.

3. Spread with a layer of tomatoes and basil followed by a layer of pasta, potatoes, olives, onion, and oregano. Repeat, seasoning each layer with a little salt and pepper, until all the tomatoes, basil, pasta, potatoes, olives, onion, and oregano are in the casserole.

4. Mix the cheese, bread crumbs, and pine nuts in a small bowl and sprinkle over the top. Drizzle with the remaining oil.

5. Cover the dish and bake for 1 hour, or until the pasta and potatoes are tender. Serve hot.

AMOUNT PER SERVING	786	24g	38g	8g	94g	2.6g
NUTRITION FACTS	CALORIES	PROTEIN	FAT	FIBER	CARBS	SALT
PERCENT DAILY VALUES (based on 2000 calories)	38%	52%	47%	32%	72%	42%

If you liked this recipe, you will love these as well.

spinach-stuffed pasta shells
with tomato sauce

212

spinach & ricotta cannelloni
with tomato sauce

214

baked rigatoni with ham & mushrooms

For an alternative version of this dish, omit the Béchamel sauce and put the cooked pasta with the mushrooms and ham in an ovenproof dish. Add 1 cup (200 g) ricotta cheese, pour over 1 cup (250 g) whipping cream, and bake for 20 minutes at the same temperature.

Serves 6

25 minutes

45 minutes

2

BECHAMEL SAUCE

3	tablespoons butter
3	tablespoons all-purpose (plain) flour
2	cups (500 ml) semi-skimmed milk
1/3	cup (40 g) freshly grated Parmesan

TO BAKE

3	tablespoons butter
1/2	cup (60 g) freshly grated Parmesan cheese
5	ounces (150 g) white mushrooms, thinly sliced
3/4	cup (90 g) diced ham
1	pound (500 g) rigatoni
5	ounces (150 g) prosciutto, cut into thin strips

1. **Preheat** the oven to 400°F (200°C/gas 6). Butter a large baking dish.

2. **To prepare the Béchamel sauce,** melt the butter in a medium saucepan over low heat. Whisk in the flour, then gradually add the milk, stirring all the time. Simmer until thickened. Stir in the Parmesan and set aside.

3. **To bake,** melt 2 tablespoons of butter in a frying pan over medium heat. Add the mushrooms, and sauté until pale gold, about 5 minutes.

4. **Add** the ham and sauté until crisp, about 5 minutes.

5. **Meanwhile,** cook the pasta in a large pot of salted boiling water until just al dente, 8–10 minutes. Drain and place half in the baking dish. Top with half the mushrooms and ham.

6. **Cover** with half the Béchamel. Make a second layer with the pasta, mushrooms, ham, and Béchamel.

7. **Sprinkle** with the Parmesan and dot with the remaining 1 tablespoon butter. Bake for 10–15 minutes until the surface is golden brown. Serve hot.

AMOUNT PER SERVING	588	30g	21g	3g	74g	2.2g
NUTRITION FACTS	CALORIES	PROTEIN	FAT	FIBER	CARBS	SALT
PERCENT DAILY VALUES (based on 2000 calories)	28%	65%	26%	12%	57%	40%

If you liked this recipe, you will love these as well.

pappardelle with sausage & mushrooms
68

tortellini with woodcutters' sauce
98

baked fusilli with tomatoes & cheese
220

baked fusilli with tomatoes & cheese

Fusilli is a perfect pasta shape to serve with heavy sauces or bakes such as this recipe. Serve with a hearty Italian red wine.

 Serves 6

 30 minutes

15 minutes

45 minutes

2

1/3	cup (90 ml) extra-virgin olive oil
1	clove garlic, lightly crushed but whole
1/2	red onion, thinly sliced
4	ounces (125 g) prosciutto, finely chopped
	Leaves from 1 bunch fresh parsley, finely chopped
	Leaves from 1 bunch fresh basil, finely chopped
6	large tomatoes, peeled and chopped
	Salt and freshly ground black pepper
1	pound (500 g) fusilli or rotini Meat Sauce (see page 208)
1/2	cup (60 g) freshly grated pecorino cheese

1. Heat 3 tablespoons of oil in a medium saucepan over low heat. Add the onion and garlic and sauté until softened, about 5 minutes.

2. Add the prosciutto, parsley, basil, and tomatoes and season with salt and pepper. Simmer until the tomatoes have broken down, 15–20 minutes. Purée in a food processor. Set aside.

4. Cook the pasta in a large pot of salted boiling water until al dente. Drain well.

5. Drizzle the remaining oil over the pasta. Season with pepper.

6. Preheat the oven to 400°F (200°C/gas 6).

7. Spoon half the pasta into an oiled baking dish, top with half the meat sauce, and sprinkle with half the pecorino. Cover with the remaining pasta, meat sauce, and pecorino.

8. Bake for 10–15 minutes, until golden brown. Let stand for 15 minutes before serving.

AMOUNT PER SERVING	1000 CALORIES	35g PROTEIN	83g FAT	5g FIBER	69g CARBS	2g SALT
NUTRITION FACTS PERCENT DAILY VALUES (based on 2000 calories)	50%	76%	95%	20%	53%	37%

If you liked this recipe, you will love these as well.

baked rigatoni with ham & mushrooms

218

baked spaghetti with chicken & spinach

314

Long
Pasta

spaghetti with garlic, chile & oil

This is a classic pasta dish. Vary the amount of oil, garlic, and chile to your liking.

 Serves 6

 5 minutes

10–12 minutes

1	pound (500 g) spaghetti
½	cup (125 ml) extra-virgin olive oil
6	cloves garlic, finely chopped

2	dried chiles, crumbled
6	tablespoons finely chopped fresh parsley

 1

1. **Cook** the spaghetti in a large pot of salted boiling water until al dente.

2. **While the pasta is cooking,** heat the oil in a large frying pan over medium heat. Sauté the chile and garlic until the garlic is pale gold, about 3 minutes.

3. **Drain** the pasta and add to the frying pan. Sprinkle with the parsley and toss over medium heat for 2 minutes. Serve hot.

AMOUNT PER SERVING **NUTRITION FACTS** PERCENT DAILY VALUES (based on 2 000 calories)	473 CALORIES 23%	10g PROTEIN 22%	22g FAT 27%	3g FIBER 12%	62g CARBS 48%	0.1g SALT 2%

If you liked this recipe, you will love these as well.

homemade **spaghetti** with garlic & oil
54

homemade **spaghetti** with tomato & garlic sauce
56

spaghetti with ricotta & pecorino

Ricotta salata is made by adding salt to fresh ricotta and then aging it for several months. It is very good for grating over pasta dishes.

 Serves 6

 10 minutes

 10–12 minutes

 1

1	cup (250 g) fresh ricotta cheese, drained
1/3	cup (90 g) butter, diced
1/2	cup (60 g) freshly grated ricotta salata cheese (or other tasty aged grating cheese)

1	dried chile, crumbled
	Salt
1	pound (500 g) spaghetti
1/2	cup (60 g) freshly grated pecorino cheese

1. **Cook** the pasta a large pot of salted boiling water until al dente.

2. **While the pasta is cooking,** mix the fresh ricotta, butter, ricotta salata, chile, and salt in a large bowl.

3. **Drain** the pasta, reserving 2 tablespoons of cooking water. Add to the bowl with the ricotta mixture and reserved cooking water. Toss well, sprinkle with pecorino, and serve hot.

AMOUNT PER SERVING	540	21g	24g	2g	63g	0.7g
NUTRITION FACTS	CALORIES	PROTEIN	FAT	FIBER	CARBS	SALT
PERCENT DAILY VALUES (based on 2000 calories)	26%	46%	30%	8%	48%	12%

If you liked this recipe, you will love these as well.

three cheese penne

170

spaghetti with zucchini

246

spaghetti with walnut pesto

This nutty pesto is also good with potato gnocchi, on crostini, in panini, or stirred into vegetarian risotto just before serving.

 Serves 6

10 minutes

10–12 minutes

 1

1   pound (500 g) spaghetti

PESTO

1   large bunch fresh basil leaves + whole leaves, to garnish

2   cloves garlic

15 walnuts, shelled

3   tablespoons pine nuts

½   cup (125 ml) extra-virgin olive oil

½   cup (60 g) freshly grated pecorino cheese

Salt and freshly ground black pepper

1. **Cook** the spaghetti in a large pot of salted boiling water until al dente.

2. **To prepare the pesto,** chop the basil, garlic, walnuts, and pine nuts in a food processor. Gradually add the oil, processing until smooth.

3. **Stir in** the cheese and season with salt and pepper.

4. **Drain** the pasta and transfer to a heated serving bowl. Add the pesto and toss gently. Serve hot, garnished with the whole basil leaves.

AMOUNT PER SERVING NUTRITION FACTS PERCENT DAILY VALUES (based on 2000 calories)	645 CALORIES 31%	17g PROTEIN 37%	38g FAT 47%	3g FIBER 12%	62g CARBS 48%	0.2g SALT 3%

If you liked this recipe, you will love these as well.

tagliolini with almond & basil pesto

32

fettuccine with pine nut & walnut pesto

38

ruote with pesto & cherry tomatoes

152

spaghetti with mediterranean pesto

This is a traditional Sicilian sauce. Caperberries are available at gourmet food stores.

Serves 6

15 minutes

10–12 minutes

1

4	large ripe tomatoes, peeled and chopped
2	tablespoons salt-cured capers, rinsed
⅔	cup (60 g) blanched almonds
1	tablespoon finely chopped fresh mint
3	tablespoons finely chopped fresh parsley
1	tablespoon finely chopped fresh basil

2	cloves garlic, peeled
½	fresh red chile, seeded and finely chopped
⅓	cup (90 ml) extra-virgin olive oil
	Salt
1	pound (500 g) cherry tomatoes, halved
1	pound (500 g) spaghetti
	Caperberries, to garnish

1. **Chop** the large tomatoes, capers, almonds, mint, parsley, basil, 1 clove of garlic, chile, and half the oil in a food processor until smooth. Season with salt.

2. **Slice** the remaining garlic. Heat the remaining oil in a large frying pan over medium heat and sauté the garlic and cherry tomatoes until the tomatoes have softened, about 5 minutes,

3. **Cook** the pasta in a large pot of salted boiling water until al dente. Drain and add to the cherry tomatoes. Add the pesto and toss well. Garnish with the caperberries and serve hot.

AMOUNT PER SERVING	495	13g	21g	5g	67g	0.1g
NUTRITION FACTS	CALORIES	PROTEIN	FAT	FIBER	CARBS	SALT
PERCENT DAILY VALUES (based on 2 000 calories)	24%	28%	26%	20%	52%	2%

If you liked this recipe, you will love these as well.

fettuccine with grilled tomato sauce

40

penne with tomatoes & goat cheese

156

fusilli with ricotta & dried tomatoes

164

spaghetti with lemon & olives

This dish is the epitome of Italian cuisine—simple, but reliant on the best, and freshest, of ingredients. The simple yet elegant sauce will only work if you use the finest quality cold-pressed extra-virgin olive oil. This sauce is also very good with whole-wheat (wholemeal) spaghetti.

Serves 6

10 minutes

10–12 minutes

1

½ cup (125 ml) extra-virgin olive oil
Zest of 2 lemons, cut into julienne strips
Freshly squeezed juice of 2 lemons
1½ cups (150 g) pitted black olives, coarsely chopped

2 cloves garlic, finely chopped
16 basil leaves, torn
Salt and freshly ground black pepper
1 pound (500 g) spaghetti

1 **Whisk** the oil, lemon zest, lemon juice, black olives, garlic, and basil in a large bowl. Season with salt and pepper.

2. **Cook** the pasta in a pot of salted boiling water until al dente. Drain well and add to the bowl with the sauce. Toss well and serve hot.

AMOUNT PER SERVING	480 CALORIES	10g PROTEIN	23g FAT	3g FIBER	62g CARBS	1.3g SALT
NUTRITION FACTS PERCENT DAILY VALUES (based on 2000 calories)	23%	22%	28%	12%	48%	24%

If you liked this recipe, you will love these as well.

ravioli with olive pesto

90

farfalle with cherry tomatoes & olives

114

whole-wheat spaghetti with spicy sauce

52

spaghetti with kiwi fruit

Kiwi fruit are another of nature's superfoods. They contain twice as much vitamin C as oranges and have high levels of potassium and lutein (which is believed to promote healthy eyes).

Serves 4

15 minutes

15 minutes

1

1	pound (500 g) spaghetti
6	kiwi fruit
1	cup (250 ml) plain yogurt
2	cloves garlic, finely chopped
1	tablespoon finely grated lemon zest
	Salt and freshly ground black pepper

1. **Cook** the pasta in a large pot of salted boiling water until al dente.

2. **While the pasta is cooking,** peel the kiwi fruit and chop three of them coarsely. Mash the remaining kiwi with a fork.

3. **Warm** the yogurt in a small saucepan over low heat. Add the garlic, chopped kiwi fruit, and lemon zest. Season with salt and pepper.

4. **Cook** over medium heat for 2–3 minutes, stirring constantly. Remove from the heat and add the mashed kiwis.

5. **Drain** the pasta and toss with the sauce. Serve immediately.

AMOUNT PER SERVING	333	13g	2g	3g	70g	0.1g
NUTRITION FACTS	CALORIES	PROTEIN	FAT	FIBER	CARBS	SALT
PERCENT DAILY VALUES (based on 2 000 calories)	16%	28%	2%	12%	54%	2%

If you liked this recipe, you will love these as well.

grapefruit **pasta salad**

118

penne with seafood & orange

176

whole-wheat spaghetti
with gorgonzola

Before aging, Gorgonzola is soft and sweet. As it ages, it becomes firmer and crumblier with a spicier taste. Use either type in this dish, depending on what you like.

Serves 6

10 minutes

15 minutes

1	pound (500 g) whole-wheat (wholemeal) spaghetti
1/4	cup (60 g) butter
8	ounces (250 g) Gorgonzola cheese, cut into small cubes

1/3	cup (90 ml) milk
	Salt
1	large ripe pear, peeled, cored, and cut into small cubes

1

1. **Cook** the pasta in a large pot of salted boiling water until al dente.

2. **While the pasta is cooking,** melt the butter in a medium saucepan over low heat. Add the Gorgonzola and milk. Season with salt.

3. **Stir** with a wooden spoon until the cheese has melted. Add the pear and mix well.

4. **Drain** the pasta and transfer to a large, heated serving bowl. Add the sauce and toss well. Serve hot.

AMOUNT PER SERVING **NUTRITION FACTS** PERCENT DAILY VALUES (based on 2 000 calories)	532 CALORIES 26%	21g PROTEIN 46%	25g FAT 31%	8g FIBER 32%	58g CARBS 45%	1.2g SALT 22%

If you liked this recipe, you will love these as well.

penne with gorgonzola

166

three-cheese penne

170

spaghetti with yogurt & avocado

Avocados are rich in heart-healthy monounsaturated fat. They have more protein and B, E, and K vitamins than any other fruit. Avocados are believed to lower cholesterol and help relieve the symptoms of arthritis.

 Serves 6

 30 minutes

15 minutes

 1

1	pound (500 g) spaghetti
¼	cup (60 ml) extra-virgin olive oil
2	cloves garlic, finely chopped
1	large onion, chopped
¼	cup (60 ml) extra-virgin olive oil
1	tablespoon dry white wine
1	ripe avocado, peeled, pitted, and diced
	Freshly squeezed juice of 1 lemon

1	cup (250 ml) plain yogurt
	Salt and freshly ground black pepper
1	fresh red chile, seeded and thinly sliced
1	celery heart, thinly sliced
1½	tablespoons salt-cured capers, rinsed
1	tablespoon finely chopped fresh parsley

1. **Cook** the pasta in a large pot of salted boiling water until al dente.

2. **While the pasta is cooking**, heat 2 tablespoons of oil in a frying pan over medium heat. Add the garlic and onion and sauté until pale gold, 3–5 minutes. Add the wine and simmer until evaporated.

3. **Drizzle** the avocado with the lemon juice to prevent it from browning.

4. **Beat** the yogurt with the remaining oil in a large bowl. Season with salt and pepper. Add the chile, celery, capers, and parsley.

5. **Drain** the pasta and toss in the yogurt sauce. Add the onion mixture and avocado, toss again, and serve hot.

AMOUNT PER SERVING	446	13g	16g	4g	68g	0.1g
NUTRITION FACTS	CALORIES	PROTEIN	FAT	FIBER	CARBS	SALT
PERCENT DAILY VALUES (based on 2 000 calories)	21%	28%	20%	16%	52%	2%

If you liked this recipe, you will love these as well.

whole-wheat penne with tuna, avocado & fresh herbs

180

farfalle with yogurt sauce & avocado

142

linguine with pesto, potatoes & beans

If the potatoes are very small, you can boil them whole. Don't peel them; they just require a quick scrub to remove any soil. You can also use small red potatoes, for extra color.

 Serves 6

 15 minutes

 15 minutes

14 ounces (400 g) green beans, chopped

1 pound (500 g) linguine

8 new potatoes, cut into ½-inch (1-cm) cubes
Pesto (see page 150)

Freshly ground black pepper

¼ cup (30 g) shaved Parmesan cheese

Sprigs of basil, to garnish

2

1. **Cook** the green beans in a large pot of salted boiling water until just tender, 4–6 minutes. Drain well.

2. **Cook** the linguine in a large pot of salted boiling water for 5 minutes. Add the potatoes and cook until the pasta is al dente and the potatoes are tender, about 5–7 minutes more.

3. **Drain well**, reserving 3 tablespoons of the cooking water, and transfer to a large serving bowl with the beans.

4. **Add** the reserved cooking water to the pesto. Spoon over the pasta mixture and toss well. Season with pepper. Sprinkle with the Parmesan, garnish with basil sprigs, and serve hot.

AMOUNT PER SERVING NUTRITION FACTS PERCENT DAILY VALUES (based on 2000 calories)	427 CALORIES 21%	14g PROTEIN 30%	17g FAT 21%	4g FIBER 16%	60g CARBS 46%	0.2g SALT 3%

If you liked this recipe, you will love these as well.

pasta with tomatoes, ricotta & pesto
144

spirals with beans & pesto
150

spaghetti with walnut pesto
228

spaghetti with zucchini flowers

Delicate zucchini flowers can be difficult to find, but check out local farmers' markets. Alternatively, if you have a garden, plant zucchini and grow your own flowers and vegetables.

 Serves 6

30 minutes

30 minutes

1

20	zucchini (courgette) flowers
1	red onion
1	small bunch fresh parsley
1/4	cup (60 ml) extra-virgin olive oil
	Salt and freshly ground black pepper

	Pinch of saffron threads mixed with 1 tablespoon warm water
3/4	cup (180 ml) beef stock
1	pound (500 g) spaghetti
1	large egg yolk
1/2	cup (60 g) freshly grated pecorino cheese

1. **Finely chop** 16 zucchini flowers with the onion and parsley.

2. **Heat** the oil in a large frying pan over medium heat. Add zucchini flower mixture and sauté for 2–3 minutes.

3. **Season** with salt and pepper and add the saffron mixture. Simmer for 15–20 minutes over low heat, stirring often and adding stock if the mixture becomes too thick.

4. **Meanwhile,** cook the pasta in a large pot of salted boiling water until al dente. Drain and transfer to the pan with the sauce.

5. **Stir in** the egg yolk and 2 tablespoons of stock. Toss over low heat, stirring constantly, until the egg mixture has set and is cooked.

6. **Sprinkle** with pecorino. Chop the remaining zucchini flowers and sprinkle over the top. Serve hot.

AMOUNT PER SERVING	547	14g	14g	4g	61g	0.4g
NUTRITION FACTS	CALORIES	PROTEIN	FAT	FIBER	CARBS	SALT
PERCENT DAILY VALUES (based on 2 000 calories)	26%	30%	17%	20%	47%	7%

If you liked this recipe, you will love these as well.

baked pasta with quails' eggs

102

penne with raw zucchini, pecorino & mint

134

whole-wheat spaghetti with onion, zucchini & basil

268

spaghetti with pea pesto

This recipe calls for garden fresh peas. Make it in early summer when tender green peas first come into the markets.

Serves 6

20 minutes

20 minutes

1

8	ounces (250 g) shelled fresh peas (about 2 pounds/1 kg) in their pods)
3	cloves garlic, finely chopped
2	tablespoons pine nuts, toasted
½	cup (60 g) Parmesan cheese, coarsely chopped + extra, freshly grated, to serve
2	sprigs fresh mint
⅓	cup (90 ml) extra-virgin olive oil
	Salt and freshly ground black pepper
1	pound (500 g) spaghetti

1. **Cook** the peas in salted boiling water until just tender, 2–3 minutes. Drain well.

2. **Combine** the peas in a food processor with the garlic, pine nuts, Parmesan, mint, and oil. Season with salt and pepper, then pulse briefly until the ingredients are coarsely chopped.

3. **Meanwhile,** cook the spaghetti in a large pot of salted boiling water until al dente. Drain well, reserving some of the cooking water.

4. **Transfer** the spaghetti to a large serving bowl and add the pesto and enough of the reserved cooking water to make a moist sauce. Serve hot, with the extra Parmesan.

AMOUNT PER SERVING	500	17g	21g	5g	66g	0.2g
NUTRITION FACTS	CALORIES	PROTEIN	FAT	FIBER	CARBS	SALT
PERCENT DAILY VALUES (based on 2 000 calories)	25%	37%	26%	20%	51%	3%

If you liked this recipe, you will love these as well.

tortellini with fava beans

100

penne with raw zucchini, pecorino & mint

134

spaghetti with zucchini

Choose small zucchini that are firm to the touch with a glossy, unblemished skin. Avoid any soft, squishy zucchini.

 Serves 6

 10 minutes

 20 minutes

 1

2	cups (500 ml) olive oil, for frying
4	medium zucchini (courgettes), thinly sliced lengthwise
	Salt
1	pound (500 g) spaghetti

⅓	cup (50 g) freshly grated pecorino cheese
	Fresh basil leaves, to garnish
	Extra-virgin olive oil, to drizzle

1. **Heat** the oil in a large deep frying pan until very hot. Fry the zucchini in batches until golden brown, 3–4 minutes each batch. Drain on paper towels. Season with salt and cover with a plate to keep warm.

2. **Meanwhile,** cook the pasta in a large pot of salted boiling water until al dente. Drain and sprinkle with pecorino. Top with the fried zucchini, basil, and a drizzle of oil.

AMOUNT PER SERVING	400	15g	12g	3g	63g	0.1g
NUTRITION FACTS	**CALORIES**	**PROTEIN**	**FAT**	**FIBER**	**CARBS**	**SALT**
PERCENT DAILY VALUES (based on 2000 calories)	20%	33%	15%	12%	48%	3%

If you liked this recipe, you will love these as well.

penne with zucchini, ham & pistachios

194

spaghetti with ricotta & pecorino

226

whole-wheat spaghetti with onion, zucchini & basil

268

vermicelli with fresh herbs

Vary the herbs according to the season and what you have on hand.

 Serves 6

 15 minutes

 15 minutes

 1

1	pound (500 g) vermicelli
1/3	cup (90 ml) extra-virgin olive oil
1	onion, finely chopped
2	cloves garlic, finely chopped
2	tablespoons finely chopped fresh mint
2	tablespoons finely chopped fresh parsley
1	tablespoon finely chopped fresh sage

1	tablespoon finely chopped fresh rosemary
1	tablespoon finely chopped fresh bay leaves
1/4	cup (60 ml) brandy
	Salt and freshly ground black pepper
1	cup (125 g) freshly grated Parmesan cheese

1. **Cook** the vermicelli in a large pot of salted boiling water until al dente.

2. **Heat** the oil in a large frying pan over medium heat. Add the onion and garlic and sauté until pale gold, 3–4 minutes. Add the herbs and sauté for 2–3 minutes. Pour in the brandy and simmer until evaporated.

3. **Drain** the pasta and transfer to the pan with the sauce. Season with salt and pepper and sprinkle with the cheese. Toss over high heat for 2 minutes. Serve hot.

AMOUNT PER SERVING NUTRITION FACTS PERCENT DAILY VALUES (based on 2 000 calories)	500 CALORIES 24%	18g PROTEIN 39%	21g FAT 26%	3g FIBER 12%	64g CARBS 49%	0.4g SALT 7%

If you liked this recipe, you will love these as well.

homemade spaghetti with garlic & oil
54

penne with raw zucchini, pecorino & mint
134

spaghetti with pea pesto
244

spaghetti with arugula, garlic & chile

Make sure that the garlic doesn't burn when browning it in the oil. If it becomes too brown, it will take on an unpleasant, acrid taste that will spoil the dish.

 Serves 6

 15 minutes

15 minutes

1	pound (500 g) spaghetti
1	large bunch arugula (rocket)
½	cup (125 ml) extra-virgin olive oil

4	cloves garlic, finely chopped
1–2	dried chiles, crumbled
4–6	anchovy fillets
	Salt

 1

1. **Cook** the spaghetti in a large pot of salted boiling water for 10 minutes.

2. **Add** the arugula and continue cooking until the pasta is al dente, 1–2 minutes.

3. **Meanwhile,** heat the oil in a large frying pan over medium heat. Sauté the garlic, chiles, and anchovies until the garlic is pale gold, about 3 minutes.

4. **Drain** the pasta and arugula and add to the pan with the garlic and oil. Season with salt. Toss gently and serve hot.

AMOUNT PER SERVING	460 CALORIES	11g PROTEIN	21g FAT	2g FIBER	62g CARBS	0.3g SALT
NUTRITION FACTS PERCENT DAILY VALUES (based on 2000 calories)	22%	24%	26%	8%	48%	5%

If you liked this recipe, you will love these as well.

ravioli with olive pesto

90

farfalle with shrimp & pesto

178

spaghetti with tomatoes, arugula & parmesan

As a variation, use whole-wheat (wholemeal) spaghetti and broccoli tops instead of the arugula. You can also add a pinch of red pepper flakes to the tomatoes.

 Serves 4

30 minutes

30 minutes

2

5	tablespoons extra-virgin olive oil
2	cloves garlic, finely chopped
1	dried chile, crumbled
3	cups (750 ml) peeled and chopped tomatoes
1	pound (500 g) spaghetti
2	large bunches arugula (rocket), finely shredded
1	stalk celery, coarsely chopped
½	cup (60 g) shaved Parmesan cheese
1	tablespoon finely chopped fresh parsley

1. **Heat** the oil in a large frying pan over medium heat. Add the garlic and chile and sauté until the garlic is pale gold, about 3 minutes.

2. **Stir in** the tomatoes and simmer for 15 minutes over medium-low high heat.

3. **Meanwhile,** cook the pasta in a large pot of salted boiling water until al dente.

4. **Drain well** and add to the sauce. Add the arugula, celery, Parmesan, and parsley. Toss well and serve hot.

AMOUNT PER SERVING	649	23g	21g	5g	99g	0.5g
NUTRITION FACTS	CALORIES	PROTEIN	FAT	FIBER	CARBS	SALT
PERCENT DAILY VALUES (based on 2 000 calories)	31%	50%	26%	20%	76%	8%

If you liked this recipe, you will love these as well.

penne with cherry tomatoes

140

ruote with pesto & cherry tomatoes

152

spaghetti with tomato & lemon

This is another simple dish that you can whip up quickly yet still be assured of serving a delicious and nutritious meal. Because the sauce is not cooked, be sure to use tasty, ripe tomatoes.

Serves 6

10 minutes

15 minutes

1

2	pounds (1 kg) ripe tomatoes
1	pound (500 g) spaghetti
4	tablespoons finely chopped fresh basil + extra leaves, to garnish
1/3	cup (90 ml) extra-virgin olive oil

Freshly squeezed juice of 1 lemon

| 2 | cloves garlic, finely chopped |
| | Salt and freshly ground black pepper |

1. **Blanch** the tomatoes in boiling water for 2 minutes. Drain well and slip off the skins. Chop the flesh coarsely.

2. **Cook** the pasta in a large saucepan of salted boiling water until al dente. Drain well and transfer to a large serving dish.

3. **Add** the tomatoes, chopped basil, oil, lemon juice, and garlic. Season with salt and pepper. Toss well. Garnish with the basil leaves and serve hot.

AMOUNT PER SERVING	440	11g	16g	4g	67g	0.1g
NUTRITION FACTS	CALORIES	PROTEIN	FAT	FIBER	CARBS	SALT
PERCENT DAILY VALUES (based on 2 000 calories)	21%	24%	20%	16%	52%	2%

If you liked this recipe, you will love these as well.

penne with ricotta, zucchini & orange

154

grapefruit pasta salad

164

whole-wheat spaghetti
with summer vegetables

With whole-wheat pasta (wholemeal) and loads of fresh vegetables, this dish is packed with vitamins and dietary fiber. Vary the vegetables according to what is in season.

Serves 6

20 minutes

20 minutes

1

5	ounces (150 g) green beans, cut in short lengths	1	yellow bell pepper (capsicum), seeded and cut into small squares
1	pound (500 g) whole-wheat (wholemeal) spaghetti	2	cups (100 g) baby arugula (rocket) leaves
1/3	cup (90 ml) extra-virgin olive oil	1	tablespoon white wine vinegar
1	clove garlic, finely chopped		Salt and freshly ground black pepper
2	stalks celery, chopped		
20	cherry tomatoes, quartered		
2	small zucchini (courgettes), cut into julienne strips		

1. **Cook** the green beans in a large pot of salted boiling water until just tender, 4–6 minutes. Drain well.

2. **Cook** the pasta in a large pot of salted boiling water until al dente.

3. **Drain** well and combine in a large bowl with 2 tablespoons of oil. Toss well.

4. **Add** the garlic, green beans, celery, tomatoes, zucchini, bell pepper, arugula, remaining oil, and vinegar. Season with salt and pepper, and toss well. Serve immediately.

AMOUNT PER SERVING **NUTRITION FACTS** PERCENT DAILY VALUES (based on 2 000 calories)	430 CALORIES 21%	13g PROTEIN 28%	16g FAT 20%	9g FIBER 39%	62g CARBS 48%	0.3g SALT 6%

If you liked this recipe, you will love these as well.

lasagna stacks with pesto

106

penne with raw zucchini, pecorino & mint

134

farfalline with grilled vegetables

132

whole-wheat spaghetti
with zucchini & bell peppers

This is a great dish to serve in summer when zucchini and bell peppers are both in season and at the height of their flavors.

 Serves 6

 35 minutes

10–12 minutes

1

1	pound (500 g) whole-wheat (wholemeal) spaghetti
½	cup (125 ml) extra-virgin olive oil
1	pound (500 g) mixed bell peppers (capsicums), seeded and cut in small squares
12	ounces (350 g) zucchini (courgettes), cut in small cubes
5	ounces (150 g) ricotta salata or feta cheese, cut in small cubes
2–3	tablespoons finely chopped fresh mixed herbs (parsley, basil, marjoram, thyme) Salt and freshly ground white pepper
1	cup (100 g) pitted black olives

1. Cook the pasta in a large pot of salted boiling water until al dente.

2. While the pasta is cooking, heat 3 tablespoons of oil in a large frying pan over medium heat and sauté the zucchini until just tender, 3–4 minutes.

3. Drain the pasta and run under cold running water. Drain again and dry on a clean kitchen towel. Combine in a serving bowl with 2 tablespoons of oil. Toss gently to stop it from sticking.

4. Add the cheese, zucchini, and bell peppers to the bowl with the pasta. Season with the remaining oil, the herbs, salt, white pepper, and olives. Toss well and serve.

AMOUNT PER SERVING	530	16g	28g	8g	57g	2g
NUTRITION FACTS	CALORIES	PROTEIN	FAT	FIBER	CARBS	SALT
PERCENT DAILY VALUES (based on 2000 calories)	25%	35%	35%	32%	44%	37%

If you liked this recipe, you will love these as well.

pasta with tomatoes, ricotta & pesto
144

spaghetti with pancetta, mozzarella & eggs
282

whole-wheat spaghetti with spicy sauce
266

spaghetti with bell peppers & pancetta

This dish is perfect for meals when you don't have a lot of time but want to make something sustaining and attractive. The sauce is equally good with whole-wheat (wholemeal) pasta.

Serves 6

15 minutes

30 minutes

1

1/3	cup (90 ml) extra-virgin olive oil	2	cups (400 g) canned tomatoes, with juice
3	ounces (90 g) pancetta, chopped	1/2	fresh red chile, seeded and chopped
1	large white onion, finely chopped	1/2	teaspoon dried oregano Salt
1	clove garlic, finely chopped	2	tablespoons capers preserved in brine, drained
2	tablespoons finely chopped fresh parsley		Handful green olives, pitted and coarsely chopped
6	fresh basil leaves, torn	1	pound (500 g) spaghetti
2	red bell peppers (capsicums), seeded and thinly sliced	1/2	cup (60 g) freshly grated pecorino or Parmesan cheese
2	yellow bell peppers (capsicums), seeded and thinly sliced		

1 Heat the oil in a large frying pan over medium heat. Add the pancetta and sauté until lightly browned, 3–5 minutes

2. Add the onion, garlic, parsley, basil, and bell peppers. Sauté until the bell peppers and onions are tender, about 10 minutes.

3. Stir in the tomatoes, chile, and oregano. Season with salt. Mix well, cover, and simmer over low heat until the tomatoes have broken down, about 15 minutes. Add the capers and olives.

4. Meanwhile, cook the pasta in a large pot of salted boiling water until al dente. Drain and add to the pan. Toss over high heat for 1 minute. Sprinkle with the cheese and serve hot.

AMOUNT PER SERVING	515	18g	19g	5g	71g	0.9g
NUTRITION FACTS	CALORIES	PROTEIN	FAT	FIBER	CARBS	SALT
PERCENT DAILY VALUES (based on 2000 calories)	25%	39%	23%	20%	55%	17%

If you liked this recipe, you will love these as well.

fusilli salad with bell peppers & arugula

116

spaghetti with pancetta, mozzarella & eggs

282

spaghetti with sun-dried tomatoes

Tasty sun-dried tomatoes are a healthy food choice. They are a rich source of vitamins C and K, potassium, copper, and manganese, and a good source of dietary fiber, thiamin, riboflavin, niacin, iron, and phosphorus.

Serves 6

25 minutes

20 minutes

1

¼	cup (60 ml) extra-virgin olive oil
3	cloves garlic, thinly sliced
3	ounces (90 g) sun-dried tomatoes, soaked in warm water for 15 minutes, drained and coarsely chopped
2	cups (400 g) canned tomatoes, with juice, chopped
1	pound (500 g) spaghetti
12	ounces (350 g) green beans, trimmed
	Salt and freshly ground black pepper

1. Heat the oil in a large frying pan over medium heat. Add the garlic and sun-dried tomatoes and sauté until the garlic is pale gold, 3–4 minutes.

2. Add the canned tomatoes and simmer until the sauce is thick, about 10 minutes.

3. Meanwhile, cook the pasta in a large pot of salted boiling water for 5 minutes. Add the green beans and cook until the pasta is al dente.

4. Drain the pasta and beans and add to the pan with the sauce. Season with salt and pepper. Toss gently over high heat for 1 minute. Serve hot.

AMOUNT PER SERVING	463	12g	19g	4g	66g	0.5g
NUTRITION FACTS	**CALORIES**	**PROTEIN**	**FAT**	**FIBER**	**CARBS**	**SALT**
PERCENT DAILY VALUES (based on 2 000 calories)	22%	26%	23%	16%	51%	10%

If you liked this recipe, you will love these as well.

pasta squares with tomatoes & pancetta

34

pasta with leeks & tomatoes

146

spaghetti with watercress & walnut sauce

Fresh, peppery watercress, onion, walnuts, mushrooms, and whole-wheat (wholemeal) pasta—this dish is packed with vitamins, minerals, and dietary fiber!

Serves 6

20 minutes

20 minutes

1	pound (500 g) whole-wheat (wholemeal) spaghetti
3	tablespoons extra-virgin olive oil
1	onion, finely chopped
2	cloves garlic, finely chopped
2	ounces (60 g) button mushrooms, sliced
1	cup (150 g) coarsely chopped walnuts
1	large bunch fresh watercress
1	cup (250 ml) sour cream
	Salt and freshly ground black pepper

1. **Cook** the spaghetti in a large pot of salted boiling water until al dente.

2. **Meanwhile,** heat the oil in a large frying pan over medium heat. Add the onion and garlic and sauté until the garlic is pale gold, about 3 minutes. Add the mushrooms and walnuts and simmer for 4–5 minutes.

3. **Remove** from the heat. Stir in the watercress and sour cream. Season with salt and pepper. Reheat over a very low heat but do not allow the sauce to boil.

4. **Drain** the pasta and transfer to a heated serving bowl. Pour the sauce over the top, toss gently, and serve hot.

AMOUNT PER SERVING	586	17g	33g	9g	59g	0.3g
NUTRITION FACTS	CALORIES	PROTEIN	FAT	FIBER	CARBS	SALT
PERCENT DAILY VALUES (based on 2000 calories)	28%	37%	41%	36%	45%	6%

If you liked this recipe, you will love these as well.

fettuccine with pine nut & walnut pesto
38

spaghetti with walnut pesto
228

whole-wheat spaghetti with spicy sauce

Whole-wheat (wholemeal) pasta has almost three times more dietary fiber than regular pasta.

 Serves 6

15 minutes

30 minutes

1

⅓	cup (90 g) extra-virgin olive oil
2	cloves garlic, finely chopped
1	fresh red chile, sliced
6–8	anchovy fillets
1½	pounds (750 g) firm, ripe tomatoes, peeled and chopped

1	cup (100 g) black olives, pitted
2	tablespoons salt-cured capers, rinsed
1	tablespoon tomato paste (concentrate)
1	pound (500 g) whole-wheat (wholemeal) spaghetti Salt

1. **Heat** the oil in a large frying pan over medium heat. Add the garlic and chile and sauté until pale golden brown, about 3 minutes.

2. **Add** the anchovies and stir until dissolved in the oil. Add the tomatoes, olives, capers, and tomato paste. Simmer over low heat for 15 minutes.

3. **Meanwhile,** cook the spaghetti in a large pot of salted boiling water until al dente.

4. **Drain** the spaghetti and add to the pan with the sauce. Toss over high heat for 1–2 minutes. Serve hot.

AMOUNT PER SERVING **NUTRITION FACTS** PERCENT DAILY VALUES (based on 2000 calories)	440 CALORIES 21%	13g PROTEIN 28%	18g FAT 22%	9g FIBER 36%	60g CARBS 46%	1.6g SALT 29%

If you liked this recipe, you will love these as well.

ravioli with olive pesto

90

farfalle with cherry tomatoes & olives

114

penne with tomatoes & goat cheese

156

whole-wheat spaghetti
with onion, zucchini & basil

The sweet, slightly caramelized flavor of the onions melds beautifully with the whole-wheat pasta.

Serves 6

15 minutes

20 minutes

1

⅓	cup (60 ml) extra-virgin olive oil
2	large white onions, thinly sliced in rings
1	fresh red chile, thinly sliced
⅓	cup (90 ml) cold water
3	large zucchini (courgettes), cut into small cubes
	Salt and freshly ground black pepper
1	pound (500 g) whole-wheat (wholemeal) spaghetti
½	cup (60 g) freshly grated Parmesan cheese
2–3	tablespoons fresh basil leaves, torn

1. **Heat** the oil in a large frying pan over medium heat. Add the onions and chile and sauté until softened, 2–3 minutes. Add the water and simmer over medium-low heat until the water has evaporated.

2. **Add** the zucchini and simmer for 10–15 minutes. Season with salt and pepper.

3. **Meanwhile,** cook the pasta in a large pot of salted boiling water until al dente.

4. **Lightly drain** the pasta and add to the pan with the sauce. Toss over high heat until the water has evaporated, 1–2 minutes.

5. **Add** the Parmesan and basil and toss again. Serve hot.

AMOUNT PER SERVING	422 CALORIES	17g PROTEIN	4g FAT	8g FIBER	60g CARBS	0.4g SALT
NUTRITION FACTS PERCENT DAILY VALUES (based on 2000 calories)	20%	37%	5%	32%	46%	8%

If you liked this recipe, you will love these as well.

penne with raw zucchini, pecorino & mint
134

penne with bell peppers, eggplant & zucchini
126

spaghetti with zucchini flowers
242

spaghetti with squash & chorizo

Spanish chorizo is made from pork and is very hot and spicy. It gets its distinctive smoky flavor and deep red color from dried smoked chiles.

Serves 6

30 minutes

25 minutes

2

1 pound (500 g) butternut squash or pumpkin, peeled, seeded, and cut in small cubes

1 cup (120 g) chorizo (or spicy salami) cut in small cubes
Salt and freshly ground black pepper

2 tablespoons extra-virgin olive oil

1 pound (500 g) cherry tomatoes, halved
Handful of sage leaves, coarsely chopped

1 pound (500 g) spaghetti
Freshly grated Parmesan cheese, to serve

1. Preheat the oven to 450°F (220°C/gas 7).

2. Put the squash and chorizo in a roasting dish. Season with salt and pepper and drizzle with the oil. Roast for 20 minutes, adding the tomatoes and two-thirds of the sage for the final 5 minutes of roasting time.

3. Cook the pasta in a large pot of salted boiling water until al dente.

4. Drain well and transfer to a heated serving bowl. Toss with the roasted ingredients and any cooking juices from the dish.

5. Serve hot, sprinkled with the remaining sage and Parmesan.

 AMOUNT PER SERVING
NUTRITION FACTS
PERCENT DAILY VALUES (based on 2000 calories)

 425 CALORIES 20%

 16g PROTEIN 35%

 13g FAT 16%

 4g FIBER 16%

 65g CARBS 50%

 0.9g SALT 16%

If you liked this recipe, you will love these as well.

pappardelle with pumpkin & saffron

ravioli with pumpkin sauce

48

94

bucatini with amatriciana sauce

Amatrice, a small town in the rolling hills of Lazio, is the hometown of this pasta sauce. Every summer a festival is held both in Amatrice and in the beautiful Roman piazza Campo de' Fiori to celebrate this special dish.

 Serves 6

15 minutes

40 minutes

 1

8	ounces (250 g) pancetta, cut into thin strips
1	medium onion, finely chopped
2	pounds (1 kg) ripe tomatoes, peeled and chopped

1	small red fresh chile, seeded and chopped
	Salt and freshly ground black pepper
1	pound (500 g) bucatini or spaghetti

1. **Sauté** the pancetta in a large frying pan over medium heat until lightly browned, about 5 minutes.

2. **Add** the onion and sauté until softened, about 3 minutes. Add the tomatoes and chile. Mix well and season with salt and pepper.

3. **Partially cover** and simmer over low heat until the tomatoes are well reduced, about 30 minutes.

4. **Cook** the pasta in a large pot of salted boiling water until al dente. Drain well and add to the sauce. Toss over high heat for 1 minute. Serve hot.

AMOUNT PER SERVING	366 CALORIES	19g PROTEIN	3g FAT	4g FIBER	69g CARBS	1.2g SALT
NUTRITION FACTS PERCENT DAILY VALUES (based on 2000 calories)	18%	41%	4%	16%	53%	23%

If you liked this recipe, you will love these as well.

pasta squares with tomatoes & pancetta

34

maccheroni with tomatoes & speck

200

bucatini with tomatoes, almonds & fried bread

Bucatini are a hollow, thick spaghetti-like pasta. They come from central Italy.

Serves 6

15 minutes

20 minutes

1

$\frac{1}{4}$ cup (60 ml) extra-virgin olive oil

1 large onion, finely chopped

4 cups (800 g) canned tomatoes, with juice
Salt and freshly ground black pepper

$\frac{1}{2}$ cup (90 g) almonds

4 thick slices day-old firm-textured bread, cut in cubes

1 pound (500 g) bucatini or spaghetti

$\frac{3}{4}$ cup (75 g) aged pecorino cheese, in flakes

1. **Heat** 1 tablespoon of oil in a large frying pan over low heat and sweat the onion for 10 minutes. Add the tomatoes and season with salt and pepper. Cover and simmer over low heat for 20–25 minutes.

2. **Toast** the almonds in a frying pan over medium heat. Remove from heat and chop coarsely.

3. **Heat** the remaining oil in the same frying pan over medium heat and sauté the bread until crisp and brown.

4. **Cook** the bucatini in a large pot of salted boiling water until al dente. Drain and transfer to a heated serving bowl.

5. **Pour** the sauce over the top. Sprinkle with the almonds, bread, and pecorino. Serve hot.

AMOUNT PER SERVING	394	15g	16g	4g	52g	0.5g
NUTRITION FACTS	CALORIES	PROTEIN	FAT	FIBER	CARBS	SALT
PERCENT DAILY VALUES (based on 2000 calories)	19%	33%	20%	16%	40%	9%

If you liked this recipe, you will love these as well.

tagliolini with almond & basil pesto

32

ruote with pesto & cherry tomatoes

152

bucatini with eggs & artichokes

This tasty dish has enough protein, vitamins, and minerals to serve as a family meal.

Serves 6

25 minutes

30 minutes

1

¼ cup (60 ml) extra-virgin olive oil
1 onion, finely chopped
3 ounces (90 g) pancetta, thinly sliced
4 artichokes
   Salt
1 cup (250 ml) dry white wine

1 cup (250 ml) water
2 eggs
1 pound (500 g) bucatini
½ cup (60 g) freshly grated pecorino cheese

1. **Heat** the oil in a large frying pan and sauté the onion and pancetta until pale golden brown, about 5 minutes.

2. **Trim** the stalks and cut the top third off the tops of the artichokes. Remove the tough outer leaves by bending them down and snapping them off. Cut in half and use a sharp knife to remove any fuzzy choke. Slice into thin wedges.

3. **Add** the artichokes to the pan and season with salt. Sauté for 2–3 minutes. Pour in the wine and cook until it has evaporated. Add the water. Simmer until the artichokes are tender, about 15 minutes.

4. **Cook** the pasta in a large pot of salted boiling water until al dente.

5. **While the pasta is cooking**, beat the eggs in a small bowl. Season with salt.

6. **Drain** the pasta and add to the pan with the artichoke sauce. Add the egg mixture and pecorino, and toss over high heat until the egg is cooked, about 3 minutes. Serve hot.

AMOUNT PER SERVING	494	20g	16g	3g	65g	0.7g
NUTRITION FACTS	CALORIES	PROTEIN	FAT	FIBER	CARBS	SALT
PERCENT DAILY VALUES (based on 2000 calories)	24%	43%	20%	12%	50%	13%

If you liked this recipe, you will love these as well.

fettuccine with artichokes

42

pasta with goat cheese & artichokes

168

spicy spaghetti with pancetta & onion

If you like spicy food, this is the dish for you. But if you don't, feel free to leave the chiles out all together.

 Serves 6

 10 minutes

15 minutes

1	pound (500 g) spaghetti
⅓	cup (90 ml) extra-virgin olive oil
1	dried chile, crumbled
5	ounces (150 g) pancetta, coarsely chopped
1	white onion, finely chopped

1	cup (50 g) finely chopped fresh parsley
1	cups (125 g) freshly grated pecorino cheese

1

1. **Cook** the pasta in a large pot of salted boiling water until al dente.

2. **While the pasta is cooking,** heat the oil in a medium saucepan over high heat. Sauté the chile and pancetta until browned, 3–4 minutes. Remove the pancetta and set aside.

3. **In the same saucepan,** sauté the onion over medium heat until softened, about 3 minutes. Return the pancetta to the saucepan and simmer gently.

4. **Drain** the pasta and add to the sauce. Season with parsley and pecorino. Toss well and serve.

AMOUNT PER SERVING	530 CALORIES	22g PROTEIN	23g FAT	6g FIBER	64g CARBS	1.1g SALT
NUTRITION FACTS PERCENT DAILY VALUES (based on 2 000 calories)	25%	48%	28%	24%	49%	20%

If you liked this recipe, you will love these as well.

pasta squares with tomatoes & pancetta

34

fettuccine with pancetta & radicchio

82

penne with spicy tomato sauce

160

spaghetti with fried eggplant & tomato

Coarse salt is a larger grained sea salt crystal and is better for drawing liquid from eggplant than normal table salt. It is also less moisture sensitive so it resists caking and is easily stored.

 Serves 6

 1 hour

1 hour

1 hour

1

14	ounces (400 g) eggplant (aubergine), with skin, thinly sliced
2	tablespoons coarse sea salt
1	cup (250 ml) olive oil, for frying

TOMATO SAUCE

| 2 | pounds (1 kg) ripe tomatoes, peeled and coarsely chopped |
| 1 | onion, thinly sliced |

2	cloves garlic, finely chopped
1	small bunch fresh basil, torn
2	tablespoons extra-virgin olive oil
1/4	teaspoon sugar
	Salt
1	pound (500 g) spaghetti
6	tablespoons freshly grated Parmesan cheese

1. **Place** the eggplant in a colander and sprinkle with the coarse salt. Let drain for 1 hour.

2. **To prepare the tomato sauce,** combine the tomatoes, onion, garlic, basil, oil, sugar, and salt in a medium saucepan. Cover and simmer over medium heat for 15 minutes. Uncover and simmer over low heat for 40 minutes.

3. **Chop** the sauce in a food processor until smooth.

4. **Heat** the frying oil in a deep frying pan until very hot. Shake the salt off the eggplant and fry in small batches until tender, 5–7 minutes per batch. Drain on paper towels. Keep warm.

5. **Cook** the pasta in a large pot of salted boiling water until al dente. Drain and add to the sauce. Toss well and place on four to six individual serving plates. Top each portion with eggplant and sprinkle with Parmesan. Serve hot.

AMOUNT PER SERVING	442	16g	13g	6g	71g	0.7g
NUTRITION FACTS	CALORIES	PROTEIN	FAT	FIBER	CARBS	SALT
PERCENT DAILY VALUES (based on 2000 calories)	21%	35%	16%	24%	55%	13%

If you liked this recipe, you will love these as well.

penne with bell peppers, eggplant & zucchini
126

spaghetti with sun-dried tomatoes
262

spaghetti with pancetta, mozzarella & eggs
282

spaghetti with pancetta, mozzarella & eggs

This hearty and nutritious recipe can be served as a one-dish meal.

Serves 6

15 minutes

30 minutes

2

2	large eggs
1/3	cup (90 ml) extra-virgin olive oil
3	small eggplant (aubergines), with skin, cut into small cubes
2	cloves garlic, finely chopped
4	ounces (125 g) pancetta, coarsely chopped
4	cups (800 g) canned tomatoes, with juice

1	fresh red chile, seeded and chopped
	Salt and freshly ground black pepper
4	ounces (125 g) fresh mozzarella cheese, drained and cut into small cubes
1	pound (500 g) spaghetti

1. **Bring** the eggs to a boil in a small saucepan of cold water over medium heat. Cook for 8 minutes from the moment the water reaches a boil. Drain and cool the eggs under cold running water. Shell and chop coarsely.

2. **Heat** the oil in a large frying pan over medium heat. Add the eggplant and sauté until tender, about 10 minutes. Use a slotted spoon to transfer to a layer of paper towels. Let drain.

3. **Add** the garlic and pancetta to the frying pan and sauté until lightly browned, 3–5 minutes.

4. **Stir** in the tomatoes and chile and season with salt and pepper. Simmer over low heat until the sauce is thick, about 20 minutes.

5. **Cook** the pasta in a large pot of salted boiling water until al dente.

6. **Drain** and add to the pan along with the mozzarella. Toss over high heat for 1 minute. Transfer to a serving dish.

7. **Arrange** the cooked eggplant on the pasta. Sprinkle with the chopped egg and serve hot.

AMOUNT PER SERVING	533	21g	22g	5g	66g	0.9g
NUTRITION FACTS	**CALORIES**	**PROTEIN**	**FAT**	**FIBER**	**CARBS**	**SALT**
PERCENT DAILY VALUES (based on 2 000 calories)	26%	46%	27%	20%	51%	17%

If you liked this recipe, you will love these as well.

spaghetti with fried eggplant & tomato
280

spaghetti with bell peppers & pancetta
260

spaghetti with squid's ink

Use as little or as much of the ink as you like. Cuttlefish has more ink than squid, but squid is more readily available. You can ask a fishmonger to prepare the squid or cuttlefish.

Serves 4

45 minutes

1 hour 45 minutes

3

1	pound (500 g) squid or cuttlefish
2	cloves garlic, finely chopped
1/4	cup (60 ml) extra-virgin olive oil
	Leaves from 1 small bunch fresh parsley, finely chopped
1/2	teaspoon dried red pepper flakes

1	tablespoon tomato paste (concentrate)
1/3	cup (90 ml) white wine
	Salt
1/3	cup (90 ml) hot water
12	ounces (350 g) spaghetti

1. **To clean the squid,** reach inside the body and pull everything out, taking care not to damage the small silver-gray sac—the ink bladder—located near the top of the body. Be sure to remove the transparent plastic-like quill running along the inside.

2. **Cut off** the tentacles just below the eyes. Reserve the tentacles and the ink sac and discard the rest of the innards.

3. **Cut** the bodies into small squares and cut the tentacles into small pieces.

4. **Heat** the oil in a medium saucepan over medium heat. Add the garlic and sauté until pale gold, about 3 minutes.

5. **Add** the squid, parsley, and red pepper flakes. Cover and simmer over low heat for 45 minutes.

6. **Pour** half the wine into a small bowl, add the tomato paste, and stir until it dissolves. Add to the saucepan.

7. **Simmer** for 20 minutes. Season with salt and add the hot water. Cover and simmer for 30 more minutes.

8. **Remove** the ink from the squid sacs, mix with the remaining wine, and add it to the sauce

9. **Cook** the pasta in a large pot of salted boiling water until al dente. Drain and add to the pan with the sauce, mixing well. Serve hot.

AMOUNT PER SERVING	537	30g	16g	3g	66g	0.3g
NUTRITION FACTS	CALORIES	PROTEIN	FAT	FIBER	CARBS	SALT
PERCENT DAILY VALUES (based on 2000 calories)	26%	65%	20%	12%	51%	6%

spaghetti with tuna & capers

This dish looks very impressive but can be prepared in just a few minutes, making it ideal for an after-work dinner.

 Serves 4

10 minutes

15 minutes

1

1	cup (100 g) salt-cured capers
8	ounces (250 g) tuna packed in oil, drained
	Leaves from 1 bunch fresh mint
½	teaspoon dried red pepper flakes (optional)
3	tablespoons extra-virgin olive oil
	Salt
1	pound (500 g) spaghetti

1. **Rinse** the capers under cold running water and cover with fresh water in a small saucepan. Place over medium heat. Bring to a boil, then drain, rinse again, and pat dry on paper towels.

2. **Combine** the capers, tuna, mint, and red pepper flakes, if using, in a large bowl with the oil. Season with salt.

3. **Cook** the pasta in a large pot of salted boiling water until al dente. Add 3 tablespoons of cooking water to the sauce to make a creamy consistency.

4. **Drain** the pasta and toss with the tuna sauce. Serve hot.

AMOUNT PER SERVING	600 CALORIES	30g PROTEIN	13g FAT	4g FIBER	96g CARBS	0.1g SALT
NUTRITION FACTS PERCENT DAILY VALUES (based on 2000 calories)	29%	65%	16%	16%	74%	2%

If you liked this recipe, you will love these as well.

pasta salad with tuna & olives
128

pasta salad with fresh tuna
130

pasta with tuna sauce
182

spaghetti with clams

If you don't like spicy dishes, leave the chile out of this recipe.

Serves 6

20 minutes

1 hour

30 minutes

1

2 pounds (1 kg) clams, in shell
¼ cup (60 ml) extra-virgin olive oil
6 cloves garlic, finely chopped
1 fresh red chile, seeded and chopped

6 large tomatoes, sliced
⅓ cup (90 ml) dry white wine
Salt
1 pound (500 g) spaghetti
3 tablespoons finely chopped fresh parsley

1. **Soak** the clams in a large bowl of cold water for 1 hour

2. **Put** the clams in a large pan over medium heat with a little water. Cover and cook until they open, 5–10 minutes. Shake the pan as they cook. Discard any clams that do not open. Remove from the heat and discard most of the shells, leaving just a few in their shells to garnish.

3. **Heat** the oil in a large frying pan over medium heat. Add the garlic and chile and sauté until lightly browned, 3–4 minutes.

4. **Add** the tomatoes and wine, season with salt, and simmer until the tomatoes begin to break down, 10–15 minutes. Add the clams and stir well.

5. **Meanwhile,** cook the pasta in a large pot of salted boiling water until al dente. Drain and add to the pan with the clams. Toss over high heat for 2 minutes. Sprinkle with the parsley and serve hot.

AMOUNT PER SERVING	510 CALORIES	33g PROTEIN	13g FAT	4g FIBER	66g CARBS	0.2g SALT
NUTRITION FACTS PERCENT DAILY VALUES (based on 2000 calories)	25%	72%	16%	16%	51%	4%

If you liked this recipe, you will love these as well.

penne with mussels

190

pasta with tuna sauce

182

spaghetti with clams, chile & arugula

290

spaghetti with clams, chile & arugula

Use small, fresh clams for best results with this dish. The soaking process is necessary to remove any sand from inside the clam shells.

 Serves 6

 10 minutes

 1 hour

 15 minutes

 1

2	pounds (1 kg) clams, in shell
1	pound (500 g) spaghetti
2	tablespoons extra-virgin olive oil
2	cloves garlic, finely chopped
⅓	cup (90 ml) dry white wine
1	fresh red chile, seeded and finely chopped

	Salt
4	ounces (125 g) arugula (rocket)
	Parmesan shavings, to serve
	Freshly ground black pepper

1. Soak the clams in a large bowl of cold water for 1 hour.

2. Cook the pasta in a large pot of salted boiling water until al dente.

3. Meanwhile, heat the oil in a large frying pan over medium-high heat. Add the clams and garlic, shaking the pan from time to time. Add the wine, cover, and cook until the clams are open, about 5 minutes.

4. Discard any clams that do not open. Add the chile and season with salt.

5. Drain the pasta and add to the pan with the clams. Add the arugula and stir until it begins to wilt slightly.

6. Serve hot with the Parmesan and a generous grinding of black pepper.

AMOUNT PER SERVING	443	32g	8g	2g	60g	0.3g
NUTRITION FACTS	CALORIES	PROTEIN	FAT	FIBER	CARBS	SALT
PERCENT DAILY VALUES (based on 2000 calories)	21%	70%	10%	8%	46%	5%

If you liked this recipe, you will love these as well.

penne with mussels

190

spaghetti with clams

288

spaghetti with mussels

294

linguine with crab & lemon

If using canned crabmeat, be sure to pick through the meat carefully to remove any fragments of cartilage or shell as these can be nasty to bite down on.

Serves 6

20 minutes

15 minutes

1 pound (500 g) linguine

⅓ cup (90 ml) extra-virgin olive oil

3 cloves garlic, finely chopped

1 fresh red chile, seeded and finely chopped

8 ounces (250 g) fresh cooked crabmeat or canned crabmeat, drained

½ cup (125 ml) dry white wine

Salt and freshly ground black pepper

4 tablespoons finely chopped fresh parsley

Finely grated zest of 1 lemon

1. **Cook** the pasta in a large pot of salted boiling water until al dente.

2. **While the pasta is cooking,** heat 3 tablespoons of oil in a large frying pan over medium heat. Add the garlic and chile and sauté until the garlic is pale gold, about 3 minutes.

3. **Add** the crabmeat and wine, season with salt and pepper, and sauté until heated through, 2–3 minutes.

4. **Drain** the pasta and add to the pan with the crabmeat. Drizzle with the remaining oil, and sprinkle with the parsley and lemon zest. Toss well and serve hot.

AMOUNT PER SERVING	423	10g	15g	3g	62g	0.1g
NUTRITION FACTS	CALORIES	PROTEIN	FAT	FIBER	CARBS	SALT
PERCENT DAILY VALUES (based on 2000 calories)	20%	22%	19%	12%	48%	2%

If you liked this recipe, you will love these as well.

penne with seafood & orange

176

spaghetti with lobster

296

spaghetti with vodka & caviar

300

spaghetti with mussels

Mussels sometimes have "beards" or weedy growths attached to their shells. You can scrub this off with a wire brush or remove it with a knife. Discard any mussels with broken shells.

 Serves 4

15 minutes

30 minutes

1

2	pounds (1 kg) mussels
1/3	cup (90 ml) dry white wine
1/2	cup (125 ml) extra-virgin olive oil
4–6	cloves garlic, finely chopped
1	large bunch fresh parsley, finely chopped

Salt and freshly ground black pepper

1   pound (500 g) spaghetti

1. **Soak** the mussels in a large bowl of cold water for 1 hour. Scrub off any beards.

2. **Put** the mussels in a large saucepan, drizzle with the wine, and cook over medium-high heat until they open up, 5–10 minutes, shaking the pot occasionally. Discard any that do not open.

3. **Strain** the mussel liquid and set aside. Remove the mussels from their shells.

4. **Heat** the oil in a large frying pan over medium heat and sauté the garlic,

parsley, and shelled mussels for 4–5 minutes. Season with salt and pepper. Remove the mussel mixture and set aside covered with a plate to keep warm.

5. **Cook** the pasta in a large pot of salted boiling water until not quite al dente.

6. **Add** the strained mussel liquid to the frying pan used to sauté the mussels and bring to a boil.

7. **Drain** the pasta and finish cooking in the boiling mussel liquid. Add all the mussels, toss well, and serve hot.

AMOUNT PER SERVING						
NUTRITION FACTS	510 CALORIES	18g PROTEIN	22g FAT	3g FIBER	64g CARBS	0.4g SALT
PERCENT DAILY VALUES (based on 2 000 calories)	25%	39%	27%	12%	49%	7%

If you liked this recipe, you will love these as well.

penne with mussels

190

seafood spaghetti en papillote

302

spaghetti with lobster

Ask your fishmonger to prepare the lobster meat for you. If desired, substitute the lobster with whole shrimp (scampi) or Dublin Bay prawns.

 Serves 6

45 minutes

45 minutes

 1

¼ cup (60 ml) extra-virgin olive oil

1 onion, finely chopped

2 tablespoons finely chopped fresh parsley

12 ounces (350 g) peeled plum tomatoes, pressed through a fine-mesh strainer (passata)

Salt

12 ounces (350 g) lobster meat, cut into large chunks (meat from 1 lobster, weighing about 1½ pounds (750 g)

12 ounces (350 g) spaghetti

1. **Heat** the oil in a large frying pan over medium heat. Add the onion and sauté until softened, 3–4 minutes.

2. **Add** 1 tablespoon of parsley and the tomatoes. Simmer until the tomatoes have broken down, 15–20 minutes.

3. **Add** the lobster meat and season with salt. Simmer for 10 minutes.

4. **Meanwhile,** cook the pasta in a large pot of salted boiling water until al dente. Drain and add to the pan. Toss well.

5. **Serve** in individual dishes and garnished with the remaining parsley.

AMOUNT PER SERVING	666	36g	17g	5g	98g	0.8g
NUTRITION FACTS	CALORIES	PROTEIN	FAT	FIBER	CARBS	SALT
PERCENT DAILY VALUES (based on 2 000 calories)	32%	78%	21%	20%	75%	14%

If you liked this recipe, you will love these as well.

penne with seafood & orange

176

penne with tomato & shrimp

186

linguine with crab & lemon

292

spaghetti with seafood

Cuttlefish and squid should either be cooked very quickly or slowly braised for at least 45 minutes; otherwise, they will become tough and chewy. Here we cook them very quickly, then we remove them from the pan, to be added at the end with the pasta.

Serves 6

30 minutes

1 hour

20 minutes

2

12	ounces (350 g) clams, in shell
12	ounces (350 g) mussels, in shell
12	ounces (350 g) squid, cleaned
12	ounces (350 g) cuttlefish
12	ounces (350 g) shrimp (prawns)
½	cup (125 ml) extra-virgin olive oil
2	cloves garlic, finely chopped
3	tablespoons finely chopped fresh parsley
1	teaspoon dried red pepper flakes
½	cup (125 ml) dry white wine
	Salt and freshly ground black pepper
1	pound (500 g) spaghetti

1. **Scrub** the mussels and clams and soak them in cold water for 1 hour. Clean the squid and cuttlefish. Chop the bodies into rounds and the tentacles into short pieces. Do not peel the shrimp.

2. **Heat** 2 tablespoons of oil in a large frying pan over medium heat. Add the mussels and clams and steam until open, 5–10 minutes. Discard any shellfish that have not opened. Extract the clams and mussels from their shells.

3. **Heat** 2 tablespoons of oil in a large frying pan over medium heat. Add the garlic, parsley, and red pepper flakes and sauté for 2 minutes, taking care not to brown them.

4. **Increase** the heat to high. Add the squid and cuttlefish. Season with salt and pepper, cook briefly, then remove the squid and cuttlefish from the pan and set aside.

5. **Add** the wine and simmer for 2–3 minutes. Add the shrimp, clams, and mussels. Simmer until the shrimp is cooked, 2–3 minutes.

6. **Meanwhile,** cook the spaghetti in a large pan of salted boiling water until al dente.

7. **Drain** the pasta and add to the pan with the seafood sauce. Return the squid and cuttlefish to the pan. Toss for 1–2 minutes over medium-high heat. Drizzle with the remaining 2 tablespoons of oil. Transfer to a heated dish and serve immediately.

AMOUNT PER SERVING	468	42g	4g	3g	62g	1g
NUTRITION FACTS	CALORIES	PROTEIN	FAT	FIBER	CARBS	SALT
PERCENT DAILY VALUES (based on 2000 calories)	22%	93%	5%	12%	48%	18%

spaghetti with vodka & caviar

There are numerous varieties of caviar, but the most famous—and expensive—is Beluga.
Use hackleback roe or salmon roe, which are delicately flavored and less expensive for this dish.

Serves 6

5 minutes

10–12 minutes

1

1	pound (500 g) spaghetti
¼	cup (60 g) butter
¼	cup (60 ml) vodka
	Freshly squeezed juice of 1½ lemons
4	ounces (125 g) smoked salmon, crumbled
4	teaspoons caviar

¼ cup (60 ml) light (single) cream
Salt and freshly ground black pepper

1. **Cook** the spaghetti in a large pot of salted boiling water until al dente.

2. **Melt** the butter in a large frying pan over low heat and add the vodka and lemon juice.

3. **Stir in** the salmon and caviar. Cook over medium-low heat for 2–3 minutes.

Add the cream, and season with salt and pepper. Remove from heat.

4. **Drain** the pasta and add to the pan with the salmon. Toss well over medium heat and serve hot.

AMOUNT PER SERVING **NUTRITION FACTS** PERCENT DAILY VALUES (based on 2 000 calories)	407 CALORIES 20%	16g PROTEIN 35%	12g FAT 15%	2g FIBER 8%	60g CARBS 46%	1.1g SALT 20%

If you liked this recipe, you will love these as well.

fettuccine with salmon & peas

64

salmon ravioli with lemon & dill

92

penne with smoked salmon

174

seafood spaghetti en papillote

En papillote is a French cooking term that involves wrapping food (usually fish with a vegetable garnish) in parchment paper or aluminum foil and baking it in a hot oven.

Serves 8

30 minutes

1 hour

40 minutes

2

1½	pounds (750 g) clams, in shell	⅓	cup (90 ml) extra-virgin olive oil
1½	pounds (750 g) mussels, in shell	½	cup (125 ml) dry white wine
14	ounces (400 g) small squid, cleaned	1½	pounds (750 g) firm-ripe tomatoes, peeled and chopped
2	cloves garlic, finely chopped	12	ounces (350 g) crayfish, shelled (optional)
1	dried chile, crumbled	1	pound (500 g) spaghetti
2	tablespoons finely chopped fresh parsley		Salt

1. **Soak** the clams and mussels in a large bowl of cold water for 1 hour. Drain and set aside.

2. **Remove** the mottled skin from the squid and cut the bodies into small chunks. Cut the tentacles in half.

3. **Preheat** the oven to 350°F (180°C/gas 4).

4. **Place** the oil in a large saucepan and sauté the garlic, chile, and parsley over medium heat until the garlic is pale gold, about 3 minutes. Pour in the wine and let it evaporate. Add the tomatoes and simmer for 10 minutes.

5. **Add** the squid, clams, mussels, and crayfish, if using. Cover and simmer over medium heat until the clams and mussels open up. Remove from the heat and discard any clams or mussels that haven't opened. Extract half the shellfish from their shells.

6. **Meanwhile,** cook the spaghetti in a pot of salted boiling water for half the time indicated on the package. Drain and add to the seafood sauce.

7. **Cut** 8 large pieces of aluminum foil or parchment paper and fold each one in half to double the thickness.

8. **Divide** the pasta into eight portions and place in the center of the pieces of foil or paper, adding 3 tablespoons of cooking water from the pasta to each portion. Close, sealing well. There should be a small air pocket in each of the packages.

9. **Bake** for 12–15 minutes or until puffed up slightly. Serve the packages directly on the table; your guests will enjoy opening their fragrant packages almost as much as they will enjoy eating the contents.

 AMOUNT PER SERVING
NUTRITION FACTS
PERCENT DAILY VALUES
(based on 2 000 calories)

 555 CALORIES 27%

 51g PROTEIN 111%

 15g FAT 19%

 3g FIBER 12%

 51g CARBS 39%

 0.8g SALT 14%

spaghetti with chili

This dish is better known in some parts of the United States as Cincinnati chili. It makes a hearty one-dish meal.

Serves 6

30 minutes

2 hours

2

2	tablespoons extra-virgin olive oil
1	large onion, finely chopped
2	cloves garlic, finely chopped
1½	pounds (750 g) lean ground (minced) beef
1	tablespoon chili powder
1	teaspoon ground allspice
1	teaspoon ground cinnamon
1	teaspoon ground cumin
½	teaspoon red (cayenne) pepper
½	teaspoon salt
1½	tablespoons unsweetened cocoa powder
2	cups (400 g) canned tomatoes, with juice
1	tablespoon Worcestershire sauce
1	tablespoon cider vinegar
½	cup (125 ml) water
1	pound (500 g) spaghetti
2	cups (400 g) canned red kidney beans, drained
2	cups (200 g) freshly grated sharp Cheddar cheese, to serve
1	cup finely chopped white onion, to serve

1. **Heat** the oil in a large saucepan over medium heat. Add the onion, garlic, beef, and chili powder and sauté until the beef is browned, 5–6 minutes.

2. **Add** the allspice, cinnamon, cumin, red pepper, salt, cocoa, tomatoes, Worcestershire sauce, cider vinegar, and water. Reduce the heat to low and simmer for 1 hour 45 minutes. Stir often, and add a little water if the sauce dries out too much.

3. **Cook** the spaghetti in a large pot of salted boiling water until al dente. Heat the beans until warmed through.

4. **Drain** the spaghetti and divide among six serving plates. Ladle the chili over the top. Top with beans and sprinkle with the cheese and onion. Serve hot.

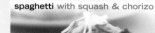

AMOUNT PER SERVING	810	48g	38g	6g	76g	1.7g
NUTRITION FACTS	CALORIES	PROTEIN	FAT	FIBER	CARBS	SALT
PERCENT DAILY VALUES (based on 2 000 calories)	39%	104%	47%	24%	58%	31%

If you liked this recipe, you will love these as well.

fettuccine with spicy chicken sauce

46

spaghetti with squash & chorizo

270

304 LONG PASTA

spaghetti with meatballs

You can make a spicier dish with the sauce on page 52.

Serves 8

40 minutes

3 hours 20 minutes

2

SAUCE

¼	cup (60 ml) extra-virgin olive oil
1	small onion, finely chopped
1	carrot, finely chopped
12	ounces (350 g) beef, in a single cut
2	pounds (1 kg) ripe tomatoes, peeled and chopped
	Salt
1	pound (500 g) spaghetti

MEATBALLS

12	ounces (350 g) ground (minced) beef
1	large egg
2	cups (250 g) freshly grated Parmesan cheese
4	cups (250 g) fresh bread crumbs
¼	teaspoon freshly grated nutmeg
1	cup (250 ml) olive oil, for frying

1. **To prepare the sauce,** heat the oil in a large frying pan over medium heat and sauté the onion and carrot until softened, about 3 minutes.

2. **Add** the beef and sauté until browned all over, 8–10 minutes.

3. **Add** the tomatoes and season with salt. Simmer over low heat until the meat is very tender, about 3 hours. Remove the meat. It can be served separately, after the pasta.

4. **To prepare the meatballs,** mix the beef, egg, Parmesan, bread crumbs, and nutmeg in a large bowl until well blended. Shape the mixture into balls the size of marbles.

5. **Heat** the frying oil in a large frying pan. Fry the meatballs in small batches until golden brown, 5–7 minutes per batch. Drain on paper towels.

6. **Cook** the pasta in a large pot of salted boiling water until al dente. Drain and add to the pan with the sauce. Toss well with the meatballs and serve hot.

AMOUNT PER SERVING	980	36g	61g	4g	77g	1.3g
NUTRITION FACTS	CALORIES	PROTEIN	FAT	FIBER	CARBS	SALT
PERCENT DAILY VALUES (based on 2000 calories)	48%	78%	75%	16%	59%	23%

spaghetti with italian sausage sauce

Be sure to use highly flavored Italian-style sausages in this simple, hearty dish.

 Serves 6

15 minutes

30 minutes

1

2	tablespoons extra-virgin olive oil
1	large onion, chopped
2	cloves garlic, finely chopped
5	Italian sausages, casings removed
4	cups (800 g) canned tomatoes, with juice

Salt and freshly ground black pepper

1 pound (500 g) spaghetti

Freshly grated Parmesan cheese, to serve

1. **Heat** the oil in a large frying pan over medium heat. Add the onion and garlic and sauté until softened, 3–4 minutes.

2. **Add** the sausage meat and sauté until browned, 5–10 minutes. Add the tomatoes and simmer for 15 minutes. Season with salt and pepper.

3. **Meanwhile,** cook the pasta in a large pot of salted boiling water until al dente.

4. **Drain** and add to the pan with the sauce. Toss well and serve hot with the Parmesan cheese.

AMOUNT PER SERVING	410 CALORIES	13g PROTEIN	14g FAT	3g FIBER	62g CARBS	0.6g SALT
NUTRITION FACTS PERCENT DAILY VALUES (based on 2 000 calories)	20%	28%	17%	12%	48%	12%

If you liked this recipe, you will love these as well.

pappardelle with sausage & mushrooms

68

festonati with italian sausages & broccoli

196

garganelli with creamy sausage sauce

202

spaghetti with stuffed bell peppers

Another hearty dish that can be served as a meal in itself.

 Serves 6

 15 minutes

70 minutes

2

6	medium green bell peppers (capsicums)	
1	large egg, lightly beaten	
½	cup (125 ml) milk	
⅔	cup soft bread crumbs	
1	onion, finely chopped	
1	teaspoon salt	
¼	teaspoon pepper	
1	tablespoon finely chopped fresh sage	

2	pounds (1 kg) ground (minced) beef
4	cups (800 g) canned tomatoes, with juice
½	teaspoon garlic salt
1	teaspoon fresh oregano leaves
8	fresh basil leaves, torn
1	pound (500 g) spaghetti
1	tablespoon extra-virgin olive oil

1. **Simmer** the bell peppers in a large pot of salted boiling water for 5 minutes. Drain and let cool slightly. Cut off the tops and remove the seeds.

2. **Preheat** the oven to 375°F (190°C/gas 5).

3. **Combine** the egg, milk, bread crumbs, half the onion, half the salt, pepper, and sage in a bowl and mix well. Add the beef and mix gently.

4. **Stuff** the peppers with the meat mixture. Arrange the peppers in a baking dish.

5. **Mix** the tomatoes with the remaining onion, salt, oregano, and basil in a medium bowl. Spoon around the peppers in the baking dish.

6. **Bake** until the peppers are tender and the meat is cooked, 45–60 minutes.

7. **Cook** the pasta in a large pot of salted boiling water until al dente. Drain and toss with the oil.

8. **Arrange** the spaghetti on six serving plates. Top each portion with a bell pepper and spoon the sauce over the top. Serve hot.

AMOUNT PER SERVING	760	42g	26g	7g	94g	0.8g
NUTRITION FACTS	CALORIES	PROTEIN	FAT	FIBER	CARBS	SALT
PERCENT DAILY VALUES (based on 2000 calories)	38%	91%	32%	28%	72%	14%

If you liked this recipe, you will love these as well.

orecchiette with roasted bell pepper sauce

86

baked penne with bell peppers

210

fried spaghetti parcels

For a lighter dish, sprinkle the molds with grated pecorino cheese and bread crumbs and bake at 400°F (200°C/gas 6) for about 40 minutes, or until golden brown. Turn out of the molds to serve.

Serves 6

1 hour 30 minutes

30 minutes

70 minutes

3

8	ounces (250 g) thin spaghetti or vermicelli
¼	cup (60 g) butter
½	cup (60 g) freshly grated pecorino cheese

SAUCE

1	cup (150 g) frozen peas
3	tablespoons water
1½	tablespoons butter, cut up
1	tablespoon finely chopped onion + ½ onion, finely chopped
½	teaspoon sugar
	Salt
3	tablespoons extra-virgin olive oil

4	ounces (150 g) ground (minced beef)
¼	cup (60 ml) dry red wine
1	tablespoon tomato paste (concentrate) dissolved in 1 cup (250 ml) boiling beef stock
	Freshly ground black pepper
½	teaspoon dried oregano
2	ounces (60 g) provolone cheese, cut into small cubes
3	large eggs, lightly beaten
1	cup (125 g) fine dry bread crumbs
4	cups (1 liter) olive oil, for frying

1. **Cook** the pasta in a large pot of salted boiling water until just barely al dente. Drain and toss with the butter and pecorino until well mixed.

2. **Oil** four 3-inch (7-cm) aluminum or soufflé molds. Spoon in enough pasta to cover the bottom and sides of the mold, leaving the center empty.

3. **To prepare the sauce,** combine the peas with the water, butter, 1 tablespoon of chopped onion, sugar, and salt in a large frying pan over medium heat. Cover and simmer until tender, about 5 minutes.

4. **Heat** the oil in a large frying pan over medium-high heat. Add the beef and sauté until browned, 7–10 minutes. Pour in the wine and let it evaporate.

Add the stock and tomato paste mixture. Season with salt, pepper, and the oregano, and simmer over low heat for 30 minutes. Stir in the pea mixture and let cool.

5. **Fill** the molds with a little of the meat sauce and provolone. Top with the remaining pasta, pressing down to seal. Let rest for 30 minutes.

6. **Carefully invert** the spaghetti forms onto a board. Dip carefully in the beaten egg, then in the bread crumbs.

7. **Heat** the frying oil in a deep-fryer over medium heat. Fry the forms, turning them once, until golden brown and crispy, 5–7 minutes each batch. Scoop out with a slotted spoon and drain and pat dry on paper towels. Serve hot.

AMOUNT PER SERVING	655	28g	40g	4g	48g	0.8g
NUTRITION FACTS	CALORIES	PROTEIN	FAT	FIBER	CARBS	SALT
PERCENT DAILY VALUES (based on 2 000 calories)	31%	61%	49%	16%	37%	14%

baked spaghetti with chicken & spinach

This is a healthy, filling dish that the whole family will enjoy. It can be prepared ahead of time and popped in the oven to bake as you come in the door.

 Serves 6

30 minutes

75 minutes

1

12	ounces (300 g) spaghetti
2	tablespoons extra-virgin olive oil
10	garlic cloves, smashed
1	red onion, chopped
4	boneless skinless chicken breast halves, chopped
4	cups (800 g) canned tomatoes, with juice
	Fresh basil leaves

1/4	teaspoon salt
1	small dried chile, crumbled
1/4	cup fresh parsley
1 1/2	cups (185 g) freshly grated Parmesan cheese
4	cups (200 g) fresh spinach
1	cup (120 g) freshly grated sharp Cheddar cheese

1. **Cook** the spaghetti in a large pot of salted until al dente. Drain and set aside.

2. **Preheat** the oven to 400°F (200°C/gas 6).

3. **Smash** 6 garlic cloves. Heat the oil in a large saucepan over medium heat. Add the garlic and onion and sauté until softened, 3–4 minutes. Add the chicken and sauté until browned, about 5 minutes.

4. **Chop** the tomatoes, basil, salt, chile, parsley, remaining 4 cloves garlic, and Parmesan in a food processor until chunky, not smooth.

5. **Add** to the chicken mixture. Simmer for 15 minutes. Remove from the heat. Stir in the spinach and pasta.

6. **Transfer** the mixture to a large baking dish. Sprinkle the cheese over the top. Bake for 25–30 minutes. Serve hot.

AMOUNT PER SERVING	548	42g	25g	3g	42g	1.6g
NUTRITION FACTS	CALORIES	PROTEIN	FAT	FIBER	CARBS	SALT
PERCENT DAILY VALUES (based on 2000 calories)	26%	91%	31%	12%	32%	28%

If you liked this recipe, you will love these as well.

fettuccine with spicy chicken sauce

44

penne with cherry tomatoes

140

spinach-stuffed pasta shells with tomato sauce

212

Index